O9-BUD-858

STRIP-PIECED
Watercolor Magic

A Faster, New Approach to Creating 30 Watercolor Quilts

Deanna Spingola

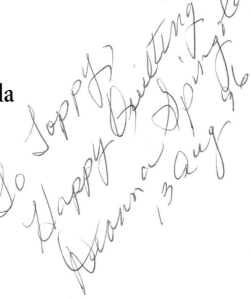

That Patchwork Place®

ACKNOWLEDGEMENTS

Many of the members of the two guilds I belong to, as well as students and quilting friends, have participated with me in this project. They have willingly tested the patterns while making many of the quilts shown in this book. I am indebted to the following people for their time, talent, and hard work:

Susan Bender, Laura Bushnell, Carol Deal, Linda Garzynski, Pamella Gray, Denise Griffin, Doris Havens, Paulette Hinton, Trisha Horner, Dorothy Larsen, Marilyn Leccese, Sheila Marie, Patricia McCormack, Martha Mueller, Katherine Noack, Camille Padilla, Karen Palese, Carol Sherwood, Tracey Steinbach, Mary Swanson, and Lorry Taylor;

My daughter, Rebecca Zafir, for the miles and miles of 2" strips that she sewed into strip sets, and for doing them in such a timely manner;

Trisha Horner, for her thoughtful advice, perceptions, friendship, and encouragement;

Deirdre Amsden, for the origin of such a remarkable concept as *Colourwash Quilts*, and Pat Maixner Magaret and Donna Slusser, who added their own impressionistic perceptions in *Watercolor Quilts*. They laid the foundation for the watercolor/colourwash phenomenon that has inspired me as well as so many other quilters;

The staff of That Patchwork Place. Surrendering this project felt a lot like relinquishing a long-awaited infant to the care of others. It was evident that this "needy newborn" required the nurturing of experienced hands to fully develop its potential, so I wisely surrendered my colicky kid to their outstretched arms. This publishing family provided patient professionalism, gentle guidance, and compassionate concern to take this project from its conception and infancy through to maturity;

Evie Ashworth and Doug Higgins of Hoffman of California, and Margaret Martin and Pat Smith of King's Road. Both companies furnished wonderful fabric.

That Patchwork Place®

CREDITS

Managing Editor	Greg Sharp
Technical Editor	Sally Schneider
Copy Editor	Liz McGehee
Proofreader	Melissa Riesland
Illustrators	Laurel Strand
	Lisa McKenney
Photographer	Brent Kane
Photography Assistant	Richard Lipshay
Design Director	Judy Petry
Text and Cover Designer	Barbara Schmitt
Production Assistants	Claudia L'Heureux
	Dani Ritchardson

STRIP-PIECED WATERCOLOR MAGIC
© 1996 by Deanna Spingola
That Patchwork Place, Inc.,
PO Box 118, Bothell, WA 98041-0118 USA

01 00 99 98 97 96   6 5 4 3 2 1
Printed in Hong Kong

No part of this product may be reproduced in any form, unless otherwise stated, in which case reproduction is limited to the use of the purchaser. The written instructions, photographs, designs, projects, and patterns are intended for the personal, noncommercial use of the retail purchaser and are under federal copyright laws; they are not to be reproduced by any electronic, mechanical, or other means, including informational storage or retrieval systems, for commercial use.

The information in this book is presented in good faith, but no warranty is given nor results guaranteed. Since That Patchwork Place, Inc., has no control over choice of materials or procedures, the company assumes no responsibility for the use of this information.

Library of Congress Cataloging-in Publication Data

Spingola, Deanna
    Strip-pieced watercolor magic : a faster, new approach to creating 30 watercolor quilts / Deanna Spingola.
        p.   cm.
        ISBN 1-56477-134-2
        1. Strip quilting—Patterns. 2. Patchwork—Patterns. 3. Color in textile crafts. I. Title.
TT835.S6384 1996
746.46—dc20   95-49071
                                                                      CIP

MISSION STATEMENT

WE ARE DEDICATED TO PROVIDING QUALITY PRODUCTS AND SERVICES THAT INSPIRE CREATIVITY. WE WORK TOGETHER TO ENRICH THE LIVES WE TOUCH.

That Patchwork Place is a financially responsible ESOP company.

DEDICATION

I dedicate this work to my two very special grandmothers: Rose Swensen Robinson (10 November 1894–3 February 1985) and Blanche Fidelia Lane Stamper (4 January 1901–28 November 1995). They each encouraged me in different ways and contributed substantially to my life.

My Grandma Robinson introduced me, by example, to the creative world of sewing and quilting. I realized at an early age that grandmothers often express not only their talents but also their love in the creative process. Although she did not actually teach me to sew because of the distance separating us, she made me aware of the possibilities; when other learning opportunities presented themselves, I was an attentive and anxious student.

My Grandma Stamper was an independent person who was forced to raise her young family alone in an incredibly difficult time. From the ages of six to ten, I was lucky enough to live down the block from her. She happily prepared a snack for me almost every day after school. She cooked wonderful holiday meals, attended open houses at my grade school, took grandchildren to the zoo, arranged Easter egg hunts, let granddaughters use her old clothes for dress-up, and was always available for her children and grandchildren. She bought the first television set in the family, and Monday evenings were spent at her house watching *I Love Lucy* and *December Bride*.

Sadly, I was informed of Grandma Stamper's death just five weeks before her ninety-fifth birthday. She was still independent and living alone and wanted very much to live to be 100. I was so eager to share this completed work with her. Just a few weeks before her death, I talked with her by phone. My last comment was, "I love you." I believe that is the most important truth I could share with her.

Both grandmothers were great role models, and they have provided me with wonderful memories. Since becoming a grandmother myself, I am reminded of the important influence the extended family can and should be.

I also dedicate this work to my loving husband, Bob, who is my wonderful companion, understanding confidant, soul mate, and best friend. We laugh at each other's jokes, share life's joys and sorrows, and more importantly, we inspire and encourage the most noble in each other.

Falling Leaves *by Tracey Steinbach, 1994, Downers Grove, Illinois, 36" x 36". Tracey used the patten for "Gabriella's Garden" on page 93, then she added appliqué leaves.*

TABLE OF

CONTENTS

INTRODUCTION

Probably no one learns as much as teachers who are planning a class or preparing a manuscript. In either case, they inevitably become aware of their own limitations and grow as a result of the increased effort expended to compensate for those limitations. Writing this book has been an excellent opportunity for me to stretch and exercise skills long forgotten, and to acquire additional ones.

As a teacher, I have never completed a class without learning something from the students. I have met many wonderful, talented, sharing, and caring people in the classroom. These associations certainly enrich my life. I am always grateful for the opportunity to share ideas and experiences with other people who enjoy the unique energy generated during the creative process.

Classes generally are (and should be) spontaneous, stimulating sessions where ideas generate ideas and everyone benefits. These spirited contemporary classrooms are probably similar in nature to the quilting bees our grandmothers and mothers may have attended. Busy women (and men) welcome the camaraderie and bonding that occurs as they share ideas, trade fabric, propose common-sense solutions to world problems, and often establish lasting friendships.

Besides a willingness to share ideas, quilters often share the work they have so lovingly created. Frequently, favorite quilts become gifts to friends and family. Quilters, as well as many others, recognize that when they give of themselves, they reap a greater reward. I hope they will enjoy and make use of the techniques in this book and continue to make the world a more beautiful place with the artwork they create.

We create quilts for a variety of reasons. Once made mostly for practical purposes, quilts have evolved into artistic expressions, manifesting our feelings, beliefs, or merely an inherent love of creativity. Many of us have a yearning to create and to feel the resulting satisfaction that elevates our sense of self.

We express love and happiness with our quilts; we also progress through periods of loss and grief during the creative process. Quilts frequently incorporate our laughter, our tears, and our poetry in color and cloth. They are much more than enhanced blankets, assembled from remnants of some previous project; they are "heart art."

As quilters, we select suitable fabric, cut it up, artfully reorganize it, and sew it back together. We make scraps on purpose. It's perfectly sane!

Quilting is a flourishing art form that requires careful planning and designing, with an emphasis on fabric, color, and value. Quilts may adorn museum walls for an appreciative audience, or they can beautify our homes for the enjoyment of our family; yet they still keep us snugly warm through a cold winter night.

How This Book Came to Be

I am a hopeless romantic and I love flowers, whether they are in a garden or printed on wallpaper or fabric. I also find quilts that have an abundance of little pieces, such as the Seminole and Bargello styles, incredibly appealing. That ultimately led to the realization that I could combine the floral fabrics and the little pieces with an easy-to-sew technique.

I began making Bargello quilts using colorful floral prints, and I was fascinated by the way they interacted. During a visit to one of my favorite fabric shops, Kathy, a conscientious employee who is aware of my floral fabric addiction, suggested a fabulous new book on a quiltmaking style that required a multitude of floral prints.

The book was *Watercolor Quilts* by Pat Maixner Magaret and Donna Ingram Slusser. This book, along with *Colourwash Quilts* by Dierdre Amsden, has inspired a whole new genre of quilts commonly referred to as watercolor quilts; in addition, it was the impetus for designing fabrics specifically for watercolor-style quilts.

Because of the vast variety of prints, particularly florals, used in *Watercolor Quilts*, my attraction to them was inevitable. I was hooked! I constructed several small wall hangings, most of them requiring more than three hundred 2" squares. I wanted to make larger watercolor quilts, but I didn't want to cut all those squares and sew them all together, one by one. As a result, I devised a faster strip-piecing method for making watercolor-style quilts. Necessity was truly the mother of invention!

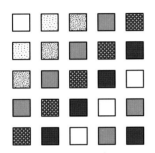

Traditional Watercolor
Cut and sew individual squares together.

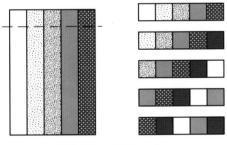

Strip-Pieced Watercolor
Use strip piecing.

Many quilters want to know precisely how their prospective quilt is going to look and exactly how much of each fabric is required. My strip-pieced method provides patterns, exact quantities, and more or less predictable results. The technique is as simple (and timesaving) as cutting strips, sewing them together, cutting them apart into segments, and sewing the segments together to make blocks. The quilts vary from contemporary to traditional. They differ from quilter to quilter as a result of individual block and fabric choices as well as quilting styles.

You can even combine this strip-pieced method with the more traditional watercolor-quilt technique. Design your one-of-a-kind work of art using 2" squares and the methods described in *Watercolor Quilts*, then coordinate its size to one or more of the design blocks in this book. Incorporate your original design within the strip-pieced blocks you select.

How to Get the Most Out of This Book

Read "Making a Strip-Pieced Watercolor Quilt" (pages 19–25) to learn the basic methods of construction. Carefully study the section on fabric selection (pages 10–18), because the ultimate success of each quilt is determined by appropriate fabric choices.

Work through the fabric-sorting exercises even if you have extensive quilting experience. These exercises will help you to develop or refine a more accurate perception of value.

If you just want to get your feet wet, rather than completely submerge yourself in watercolor, select a quilt made with a smaller five-, six-, or seven-square block, such as "Galaxy Five" (page 59), "Watercolor Rails" (page 48), or "Butterflies in the Garden" (page 89). Each takes relatively few fabrics and is less intimidating than some of the larger designs, especially if you do not already own a large stash of appropriate fabrics.

Read about appropriate fabric styles (pages 14–18), then jump in. Choose your fabrics, cut your strips, and start constructing blocks. It's that simple!

Be patient with your progress; don't worry if you make a mistake. Practice until you are satisfied with your skills. Evaluate any problems that you may encounter. Are they within your control or do they relate to the equipment used? Even the most capable seamstress can't compensate for dull rotary blades, poor-quality fabric, or a sewing machine that isn't functioning properly, so use the best fabric and equipment that you can. Set realistic, achievable goals and, most important, enjoy a pleasant, creative experience.

EQUIPMENT

You will need basic quiltmaking tools to make strip-pieced watercolor quilts.

Rotary Cutter: Olfa recently introduced a rotary cutter with a 2¼" diameter blade. This is the one I prefer. Its larger size is particularly useful when cutting through multiple layers, as in the Twelve-Square blocks. The medium-sized cutter also effectively cuts multiple layers as long as the blade is sharp. Sharp blades are a necessity, so always keep extras on hand. The small cutter is inadequate for the cutting required in strip-pieced watercolor techniques.

Cutting Mat: Use a mat that is at least 24" x 36". The mat must be large enough to accommodate the folded width of 45"-wide fabric, as well as the finished strip sets.

Acrylic Rulers: 6" x 24" and 6" x 6" are my favorite sizes. I prefer Quilter's Rule products for measuring because the ridges on the bottom help to prevent the ruler from slipping while you cut. Use the same ruler for all of the cutting, because a slight size variation may exist between different rulers or brands.

Sewing Machine: A dependable and efficient sewing machine is a necessity. Know how to clean and maintain yours, and keep it in top running condition. Check the tension by simultaneously running your thumb and forefinger along the top and bottom of a stitching line. It should be even, with no irregularities. For general piecing, use 12 stitches per inch. For the most consistent seam allowances, use the same machine throughout the entire project.

Thread: Use high-quality, mercerized, 100% cotton thread for piecing and quilting. I use tan or beige for light fabrics and gray or smoky green for dark fabrics.

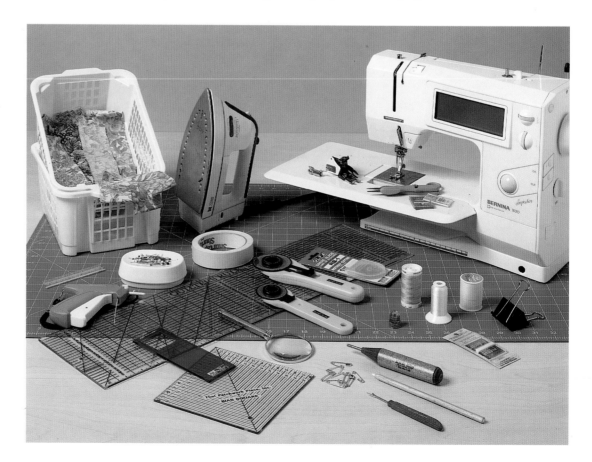

Poor-quality thread lacks uniformity and tends to be abrasive, making it hard on the sewing machine and, ultimately, on the fabric in your quilt.

Use clear or smoke-colored nylon thread manufactured exclusively for machine quilting, and use it in the top of the machine only. There are other nylon threads available but they are inappropriate for quilts. I prefer 100% cotton quilting thread in a compatible color for hand quilting.

Hand-Quilting Needles: Hand-quilting needles (called Betweens) come in sizes 3–12, but sizes 8–10 are most frequently available. A larger number indicates a shorter needle. Choose the size according to your skill level.

Sewing-Machine Needles: Use size 70/10 or 80/12 for both piecing and machine quilting. Change needles with each new project, after about six hours of continuous sewing, or when you hear the needle pop or thud into the fabric. Needle and thread sizes should be compatible. If you are machine quilting with delicate nylon thread, use a comparable needle. Specialty threads, such as metallic, require a needle with a larger eye to prevent the thread from fraying.

> *Tip* TO FACILITATE THREADING THE NEEDLE, cut the thread at a sharp angle and wet the back of the needle rather than the thread. The thread will slip right through the needle hole.

Steam Iron and Ironing Board: Use a good, clean steam iron. Pressing with steam makes the strip sets lie flatter and the seam allowances easier to control.

Safety Pins: Use medium (1½") pins to pin the blocks together after you crosscut the segments and before sewing. Use small (½") pins to mark the top left square of each finished block. I also use the medium-sized ones (1" or 1½") to pin-baste the quilt sandwich together.

Kwik Klip™: Use this handy tool to fasten and unfasten the pins. If you baste with safety pins, this tool saves a lot of wear and tear on your fingers.

QuilTak™: This remarkable little gun secures the top, batting, and quilt backing together by inserting a short plastic tab through the three layers. It makes basting much faster than basting with safety pins, and the tabs are easier to maneuver around.

QuilTak Basting Grid: Place this grid under your quilt when using the QuilTak so you can accurately aim the gun straight down through the quilt rather than at an angle. The grid prevents the needle from grazing the work surface and damaging either the needle or the surface.

Seam Ripper: Even an eternal optimist needs one of these for occasional unsewing or deseaming.

Thimble: Find one that fits comfortably on the middle finger of your sewing hand and use it for any kind of hand sewing or quilting.

Small Scissors or Thread Clippers: They are easier to use at the machine than large scissors.

Ruby Beholder®: The Ruby Beholder is a versatile little tool made of dark red acrylic. Hold it close to your eyes and view your fabrics through it to determine the value range of a group of prints. At the opposite end of the viewing section is a 1½" window. Use this when considering the motif spacing and appropriateness of a selected fabric. See page 13 for more information about using the Ruby Beholder.

Photocopy Machine: Photocopies of fabric can help you learn to recognize value and evaluate motif style. See page 13 for more information about photocopying fabric.

Design Wall: While a design wall is not essential during block construction, it is very beneficial for arranging the blocks in any style of quilts. This straight-on view of your design makes it easier to evaluate and rearrange completed blocks until you are satisfied with their arrangement. Use Thermolam®, felt, or Pellon® secured to foam-core board, rigid cardboard, or a wall. I use 72"-wide felt tacked to a wall.

Reducing Glass: This optional tool has a concave lens that reduces the size of things. (I have tried it on my hips and thighs, but to no avail. Oh well!) This little tool visually increases the distance between you and the object you are viewing, giving an entirely different perspective of the piece; value placement and pattern become more apparent. These are available at some quilt shops and art-supply stores. Get a similar view by looking through a camera lens, a door peephole (available at the hardware store), or through the wrong end of a pair of binoculars.

Six Boxes or Baskets: Organization is important. Use baskets or boxes to keep the cut and folded fabric strips arranged according to value. These baskets become your color/value palettes.

FABRIC SELECTION

A wonderful quilt is dependent upon wonderful fabric. Just as you can't make gourmet chocolate cheesecake with powdered milk, you can't expect to make a superb quilt using poor-quality fabric! For best results, always use high-quality, 100% cotton fabric.

Fabric selection for a watercolor quilt is dependent on a number of factors. These include hue, tint, shade, tone, and temperature. Value, however, has the most important role in creating the wash of color that characterizes this style of quilt.

In addition to color properties, the actual printed design must be considered when choosing fabrics. Size and style of the printed designs, visual texture, and spacing of the printed motifs are all-important properties that affect the final outcome.

Understanding Color and Its Properties

Color plays a key role in the success or failure of any quiltmaking project. Understanding the properties of color will help you plan effective fabric choices for strip-pieced watercolor quilts.

The study of color is inseparably linked to the art of quiltmaking. Though we take color for granted, our lives would be dull and monotonous without our ability to perceive color.

Color is conveyed by light, which contains all of the colors; its greatest source is the sun. When light strikes an object, the rays are mixed; then they are either absorbed or reflected. Reflected rays allow the observation of color; then the mind assigns each observation a name.

Hue: Hues are the clear, concentrated primary colors that make up the energetic pure-color scale; colors created by mixing two primary colors together are also considered hues. This brilliant, dynamic group has no altering additives, such as white, black, or gray. Combine the visually strong, bright hues of the pure-color scale with tints, tones, and shades to produce interesting watercolor quilts.

Fabric companies often print these bright, pure colors on

This color wheel presents only a fraction of the color options available.

dark backgrounds, which emphasizes the pure hues and adds an iridescent quality to the fabric.

Tint: Color tints are any of the pure hues lightened by the addition of white. White increases the value of a hue; the more white used, the lighter and more delicate-looking the fabric becomes. Red with white added becomes pink; the more white you add, the paler pink it becomes.

Shade: Add black to pure colors and they become shades; the more black added, the darker the fabric. For instance, a medium green becomes pine green when black is added. Shades are especially important to strip-pieced watercolor quilts because they provide a wonderful rich contrast as well as strength and stability.

Tone: A tone is pure color with the addition of gray (a combination of black and white). Gray dilutes the intensity and affects the brightness of a pure hue, making the color look muddy, dusty, or dull, but not uninteresting. The pure color becomes more subtle, losing its intensity. It may become a darker or lighter value, depending on the amount and value of the gray added, or it may stay the same. Use a predominance of tones to give your watercolor quilt a soft, misty look.

Beige and ecru prints are actually yellow tones. You may successfully combine them, for value purposes, with clear tints, but the tones will look dirty beside the tints. Nevertheless, because there is such a large variety of fabrics in a watercolor quilt, this difference is more acceptable than it would be in a more traditional quilt.

Temperature: Colors have long been associated with temperature. Red, orange, and yellow come to mind when we consider the warmth of the sun or a blazing fire. The coolness of blue, green, and violet remind us of foliage, sea, and sky. These are visual sensations rather than physical ones; a red and yellow quilt will not keep you any warmer than a blue and green quilt.

Warm colors (yellow, orange, and red) advance, while cool colors (blue, purple, and green) retreat. Because our eyes are drawn first to warm colors, these colors demand and usually gain our attention. Consequently, we may notice the flowers on a piece of fabric before we see the leaves that frame them. Notice the difference between the flowers printed on the blue background and those on the white background in the photograph, above right. An excellent example of a cool-temperature quilt is "Falling Leaves" (page 3), while "Cosmic Energy" (page 42) sizzles with reds.

Yellow is the color that our eyes register first. It is powerful and visually stimulating. For this reason, use yellow in moderation, as an accent rather than as the focus color.

The warm yellow flowers advance while the cool background retreats. Note the different emphasis between the blue background and the white background.

Take a lead from nature when you plan the temperature of your quilt: try combining warm and cool colors. Choose a majority of warm or cool prints, depending on the effect desired. A small amount of yellow, orange, or red added to a combination of cool prints gives a gentle radiance to a quilt. "Valerry" (page 27), "Who Knows?" (page 73), and "Aztec Treasures" (page 95) have a predominance of cool colors with a relatively small amount of warm yellow.

Value: Value is the degree of lightness or darkness in a fabric surface. A visually light fabric is high in value, while a visually dark fabric is low. A tint (white added) is higher in value than a shade (black added). The selection and position of the varying degrees of value create the contrast and provide definition and blending in a watercolor quilt.

Using Value Effectively in Watercolor Quilts

For our purposes, there are six designated values in strip-pieced watercolor quilts:

- Dark Dark
- Light Dark
- Dark Medium
- Light Medium
- Dark Light
- Light Light

The value of a fabric is relative, influenced by the neighboring fabrics. A medium-value fabric may appear light if it is placed next to dark fabrics; conversely, that same medium fabric will appear dark if it is surrounded by lights.

Fabric temperature and intensity are affected in the same way. A warm red (with a yellow undertone) advances next to a cooler red (one that has a blue undertone). A very cool blue recedes when it is adjacent to a green with a yellow undertone. A normally warm red/orange appears even warmer next to a cool color, while a cool color appears even cooler in a warm fabric environment. A toned-down fabric (with gray added) appears more subtle in the presence of pure colors, and a solitary pure color seems more intense surrounded by toned-down fabrics.

Relativity affects many areas of our lives. I used to regard people my age as old. Now I consider them in their prime. While this is not quite what Einstein meant, that's the theory of relativity in a nutshell!

The Functions of Value

The light values, combined with or placed next to the darks, provide wonderful contrast, structure, and depth in a watercolor quilt. As the light value seems to advance toward the viewer, it gives a three-dimensional effect. "Melanie's Wind Chimes" (page 45), "Aim for Lofty Heights" (page 53), "Taylor's Game Board" (page 87), "Butterflies in the Garden" (page 89), and "Celestial Starship" (page 91) are good examples of this three-dimensional effect.

The medium-value prints are the most visible in a quilt, and their visual texture is the most perceptible from a distance. Medium values are the favorite choice of many quiltmakers. Perhaps that is why there seem to be more medium-valued fabrics available than light and dark values.

Dark values provide definition and shape in a block design. These values tend to recede. It is that wonderful rich darkness, contrasted and combined with the other values, that makes such a significant contribution to watercolor quilts. Because these fabrics are dark, the print pattern is hardly visible from a distance. When you photocopy a dark-dark fabric, you will barely see the pattern. For this reason, you can often get away with less variety in the scale and color of these fabrics.

Value is relative.
The medium-value center strip appears to transform as the adjacent values change.

Value Samples. These samples demonstrate value only. Do not feel compelled to purchase these exact prints.

Value Vision

Value vision is the ability to accurately determine the value of a piece of fabric. This is an important skill when you are creating a watercolor quilt. Distinguishing value between just two fabrics might be a snap, especially if those fabrics are solids; however, multicolored print fabrics are another matter.

To determine the value of a fabric, you must totally disregard color. Sound strange? How can you define a light or dark color by disregarding it? I use the following three methods for determining value:

- Look at the fabric through a color-filtering device such as the Ruby Beholder (page 9) to provide a quick temporary view, but remember that it makes red fabrics look light and green fabrics look dark no matter how they combine with your other fabrics in reality.
- Photocopy some of your fabrics so that you can see how they look in varying shades from white to black. Study them, cut them up, and compare them to the actual fabric. Because the photocopier eliminates color, the print style and motif size become more apparent. However, the photocopier does not accurately copy some lighter blues, some reds, and some tans, so be aware.
- Look at your fabric through a reducing glass or other similar tool. Some quilters even squint to determine the value. Use the method that works best for you. You can develop a good sense of fabric value by combining these methods.

The following exercise will help you determine your personal fabric preferences. Even if you are an experienced quilter, this practical experiment will help you to evaluate and validate your current selections and, if necessary, show where you need to add to them.

Choose two prints from each of the six values listed on page 11 for a total of twelve fabrics. Make a photocopy of the value examples on page 12. Photocopy your own fabric selections. Now compare the two photocopies. Sort your photocopied fabrics according to the predominating value. Some fabrics may fit into more than one category, depending on the adjacent fabric.

Examine your assortment of prints. Are they all the same style or size? Do you need to add smaller or larger prints? Use the photocopies as a guide to help you evaluate your fabrics objectively. Don't become so concerned about the details of individual fabrics in an attempt to achieve perfection that you never make a quilt. Remember, it is not the individual fabrics, but the overall effect of the quilt that is significant.

The Pretenders

Fabrics with dark backgrounds are not necessarily dark-value fabrics. I call them "pretenders." Depending on the value of the motif and its coverage on the fabric, they can be medium or even light values masquerading as dark. These fabrics often have only a small amount of dark background showing. Be sure to sort each print according to its predominating value.

Value Pretenders. Sort fabric by the predominating value, not necessarily the background value.

The Heart block shown below demonstrates the consequences of using pretender darks. The block lacks definition and contrast. I refer to this block as my "Bad Heart" block. Compare it to the Heart blocks used in "The Hearts of the Children" (page 67). Each of the six values is represented in that quilt, and the overall design is much more dynamic and needs no explanation.

Quilt Confetti

Small- to large-scale, medium-value prints, contrasted with very light and very dark fabrics, create the wreaths and random scattering of what I refer to as "quilt confetti." "Mia Marie's Maze" (page 61) has columns of confetti, and "Valerry" (page 27) and "Calvary" (page 83) both have a wreath of confetti in the center. The style of fabrics chosen makes the wreath in "Valerry" appear more delicate.

Quilt confetti is the result of several things:
- The combination of small-, medium-, and large-scale prints
- The predominance of medium-value fabric
- The use of multicolored prints
- The small size of each individual square

The light and dark fabrics, because of their distinct values, highlight the more obvious print of the medium values. Even if you use a variety of print scales in dark or light fabric, those values will not have the same impact as the medium value. That is not their function. The large number of small, multicolored, medium-value pieces, accented by the lights and darks (quieter prints), creates confetti.

Sore-Thumb Squares

When the design requires a dark-dark print, avoid one that includes a lot of a lighter value. You may end up with a lighter-value square rather than the necessary dark-dark square, thus interrupting the pattern. This is most important when you choose dark-dark fabrics; you have a lot more flexibility using mixed-value prints when you work with light and medium values.

Contrasting Value. Avoid using a dark value that also contains a very light value.

"Spingola Spin" (page 30) is a good example of this "sore-thumb" effect. The light value in the second square from the top on the left side is very apparent against its darker-valued neighbors, although it seemed negligible when I chose the strip.

> *Tip*
>
> SOLVE THE SORE-THUMB PROBLEM with a jar of textile paint and a brush. Darken the value of a fabric by completely covering the light value with paint or by simply writing your initials or name and date in that square.

Evaluating Printed Fabrics

As you select fabrics for watercolor quilts, choose a variety of motifs to create visual texture in the finished quilt.

Texture

The design printed on a fabric gives it visual texture. When making strip-pieced watercolor quilts, I avoid solid-colored fabrics or fabrics that appear solid from a distance, especially the medium values. They become sore-thumb squares because they lack the design lines and multiple colors that shape and develop the unique look of a watercolor quilt.

Motif Sizes

A motif is the repetitive design printed on the fabric. Motifs appear in an assortment of shapes and sizes, from very small to very large; they may be printed randomly or symmetrically. To provide more contrast, texture, and interest in a quilt, use prints with a variety of motif sizes. Combine small-, medium-, and large-scale prints to give visual texture and energetic motion to the piece. Do not limit yourself to one size.

Use small, medium, and large motifs.

Motif size and style ultimately determine the mood of the quilt. Choose motifs that are appropriate for the feel or look you are trying to achieve. Small- to medium-scale florals produce a more romantic, delicate-looking quilt, such as "Valerry" (page 27), while a predominance of larger motifs or straight-line, less fluid geometric styles, as in "Calvary" (page 83), gives quite a different look. The best print styles are multicolored and densely printed. Refer to "Purchasing Fabric" on pages 16–18 for more information on print styles.

Motif Spacing

Because of the variations in motif spacing, some designs reveal more background. Fabric designs with large solid-colored areas are not a good choice for strip-pieced watercolor quilts because you do not cut individual 2" squares or selected motifs; instead, you cut whole strips of fabric. Therefore, it is better to use a fabric that has a minimum of background;

this prevents major portions of any of the squares in the quilt block from appearing as a solid fabric.

Use fabrics showing a minimum of background.

These fabrics would not be appropriate for this technique.

Fabrics with small, symmetrical motifs and some background fabric showing are satisfactory, but they tend to be static and lack some of the appealing characteristics of other print styles. They are acceptable if they are very light or very dark values, but I do not recommend them in medium values.

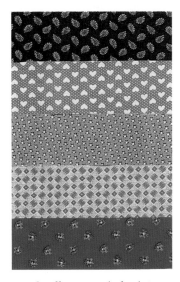

Small symmetrical prints

Transitional Prints

A transitional fabric is a print whose style lines or multicolored features make the design flow more easily from one fabric into the adjacent fabric. A print's style lines, its value, and its color determine its transitional quality.

Using fabrics with similar style lines and multiple colors makes it easier to choose a neighboring print. For instance, if you are using a fabric with yellow and purple in it, you may more easily choose one that has either color in it as the next fabric. It may be the same value, or it may be lighter or darker.

Transitional prints with
yellow and purple

Most transitional prints do not have a symmetrical design; the motifs appear to be randomly distributed. This style of print flows through the quilt more easily than static, symmetrically printed fabrics because the eye does not rest on a transitional fabric. Strips cut from a transitional fabric do not appear to be identical.

Purchasing Fabric

Many fabrics available today are appropriate for watercolor quilts. Make a statement about your personality, hobbies, background, or lifestyle through your fabric choices. Each quiltmaker's unique combination of prints lends a personal interpretation to the patterns. Following are some suggestions for prints appropriate for watercolor quilts. Many print styles are good transitional prints; some work well as very light and very dark values but do not work when used as medium values.

- Choose a large variety of colors. Focus on your favorite colors, but expand your palette to include all colors. While many people do not wear yellow, it can provide a very effective light source in a quilt. There is nothing quite like the color yellow, dancing across the surface, to brighten or warm up a quilt.

- There are no ugly colors, even though we have all seen examples of colors used in very unappealing ways. You may not like a particular color, but if a small quantity of it contributes to the composition of the quilt, then use that color. While there is security in repeatedly using colors that you like, there may also be a certain amount of sameness about your quilts. Experiment with the endless color options available to you. Use small amounts of all the colors, even those you formerly considered unattractive or even downright ugly.

- I keep a more-than-adequate supply of all the values on hand. Some people buy only the fabric that they need for each project. Others buy what attracts them, with no particular purpose in mind except that it may eventually be "The Perfect Fabric." Like many of you, I am a collector, but I purchase fabric according to its value. Quilters cannot always schedule or predict those energetic periods of inspired creativity. Rather than face frustration, have the appropriate fabrics available for those moments, whether they come at 5:00 A.M. or midnight.

- After you have sorted and organized your fabric by value, add additional fabrics to your collection as necessary. If you need an excuse to go fabric shopping, this is it!

- When you shop for fabric, establish some objectives. Remember, the main focus should be on value. Make a list so you don't become too distracted by the temptation of recent arrivals. Stock up heavily on both light and dark values in the seasons when they are more readily available. Medium values are always abundant.

- For the strip-pieced watercolor technique, buy just the minimum the shop will sell; sometimes it is as little as an eighth of a yard. Purchase fat quarters if you are making a quilt that requires only nine blocks. Only one 2"-wide strip of each fabric is required for any of the nine-block quilts in this book. If a quilt plan requires twenty-five different fabrics, you will need twenty-five different 2" strips, but buy a few extra pieces so you have more options.

- Have on hand a few more print choices than the block pattern actually requires. This greater selection allows you to choose the most suitable print from among several of a similar value. Choose from the following print styles.

Florals: The most readily available printed fabrics have small-, medium-, and large-scale multicolored floral designs. This category also includes the small traditional calico prints that our mothers and grandmothers probably used. These small prints work well in the light value, but don't make a whole quilt with medium-value, small calicoes. Use a variety of sizes.

Florals

Vegetables and Fruits: By their very nature, prints containing fruits and vegetables are colorful, transitional, random, and interesting. These prints are comparable to florals because of their color and print flow.

Vegetables and Fruits

Geometrics: These include plaids and some stripes, as well as printed designs that are geometric in nature—squares, cubes, and triangles. Because their style lines are generally straight, these prints march boldly, rather than flow gently, into the next fabric.

Geometrics

Monochromatic and Two-Color Prints: Monochromatic prints, those combining a few values of one color family, are difficult to use in watercolor because they tend to look like solids when viewed from a distance. I rarely use them except in the very dark or the very light values. Two-color prints, though similar, are marginally more usable, but again only as very light and very dark values.

Monochromatic and Two-Color

Theme Prints: Prints denoting specific holidays, such as Christmas, Easter, or Valentine's Day, can be good choices, as can fabrics featuring members of the animal kingdom or those printed with leaves, sky, rocks, feathers, or water. Sports prints and landscapes, including houses and people, are also good choices. Paisleys, marbleized surfaces, swirls, ethnic designs, and abstract or unevenly spaced multicolored dots make a nice addition to watercolor quilts.

Animal Kingdom

Landscapes

Theme Prints

Environmental Elements

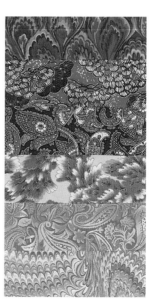

Others

MAKING A STRIP-PIECED WATERCOLOR QUILT

When you make a traditional water-color quilt, you sew small squares together in rows, then sew the rows together to complete the quilt top.

When you make a strip-pieced water-color quilt using my method, you sew strips together, cut the strip-pieced units into segments, then sew the segments together to create watercolor blocks. After assembling all the blocks, you sew them together to complete the quilt top.

Sorting Your Fabrics

Since the pattern of each design block in a strip-pieced watercolor quilt is determined by the placement of the light, medium, and dark values within the block, you must sort, evaluate, and organize all of your fabrics, or at least those fabrics that you intend to use for strip-pieced water-color. It may surprise you to discover exactly what you have been buying.

You may be able to organize your fabrics quickly, but you may need to take vacation time, stock up on frozen dinners, remove the phone from the hook, and sequester yourself in a room to do this exercise. Sort all of your cotton prints into six separate piles (or rooms), representing the six values: Light Light, Dark Light, Light Medium, Dark Medium, Light Dark, Dark Dark. When a fabric contains more than one value, sort by the predominating value.

If this sounds like a lot of effort for one quilt, consider it a learning process. Quilters love to look at and caress fabric. As you go through your fabric collection, you may find some outstanding fabrics that you have forgotten. Of course, you may also question some of your choices. This activity will also help you to become more skillful in selecting fabrics for future quilting projects.

Preparing Your Fabrics

To launder or not to launder? The answer to that question depends on what you are making and the quality of the fabrics you have selected.

Wash fabric for two reasons: to preshrink it and/or to get rid of extra dye so it will not bleed. Modern technology has greatly reduced the shrinkage factor. Better fabric manufacturers use very high-quality goods and finish them in such a manner that there is minimal shrinking and little if any bleeding. Of course, fabrics of different quality respond differently. Use your best judgment.

If you are making a crib quilt or appliquéing rich, dark colors on a light background, wash the fabric. Certain colors, such as red, blue, and green, tend to be less stable; wash those. Use warm water, never hot or cold, and mild soap, preferably the same soap that you anticipate using on the finished quilt.

To check dye stability, pin a small swatch of the proposed fabric to a piece of white fabric. Wash this fabric the same way you plan to wash the completed quilt. After the wash, if the white fabric is no longer white, the dye will probably bleed. In that case, continue to wash that fabric until the water is clear. Dry your fabrics in the dryer, which is where most of the shrinkage takes place. Or wash small pieces by hand, hang them to dry, then press them with a hot iron.

Cutting and Organizing Strips

Cut all your chosen fabrics into 2"-wide strips, across the width of 44"-wide fabric (crosswise grain). Many of the designs require only a portion of a strip; reserve the unused piece for another project.

Fold the fabric so that the selvages are even, then place it on the cutting mat with the fold closest to you. Place the bulk of the fabric to the right of the ruler if you are right-handed; if you are left-handed, place the bulk of the fabric to the left of the ruler.

Place one of the lines of the 6" x 6" square ruler on the fold of the fabric, close to the cutting edge. Now place the 24" ruler next to the 6" square. Remove the 6" square and trim the uneven raw edges away with the rotary cutter, cutting away from your body. This is a "clean cut." If you have a gridded mat, you may align the fold with one of the horizontal lines on the mat rather than using the 6" square.

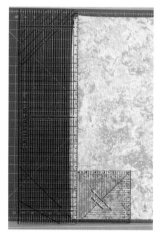 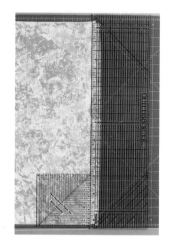

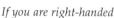

If you are right-handed   *If you are left-handed*

Walk your fingers up the ruler as you cut. The hand that is cutting should be opposite the hand that is holding and steadying the ruler. This prevents the ruler from shifting out of position as you cut.

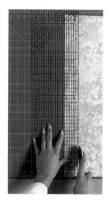  

Cut several layers at a time. For best results, limit the number of layers to twelve at the most. The large

rotary blade is extremely efficient and designed to cut multiple layers. To accurately cut multiple layers, stagger the fabrics so that ¼" of each previous layer is showing on the mat.

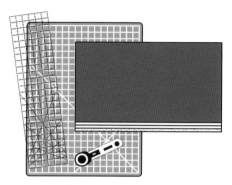

Stack and cut in multiple layers.

Be sure that all the folds are parallel; otherwise, you may end up with a crooked strip. If this occurs, cut the strip into two pieces and use each half for a project that requires a shorter strip.

Cut a crooked strip in half and use both parts.

When you cut multiple layers, hold the cutter straight up and down; if it leans to either side, the strips will be inaccurate. Fold a piece of fabric so that it is the same height as the layers being cut and place it under the opposite edge of the ruler. This levels the ruler and makes cutting more comfortable as well as more accurate.

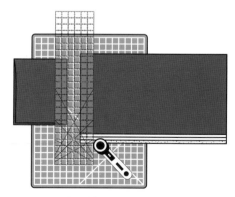

Place fabric under the other
side of the ruler to keep it level.

Fold the cut strips neatly and organize them in separate baskets according to value. If one piece seems out of place, move it to a more appropriate group. Designate a separate basket or box for each value to make it easier to choose the proper values for your chosen design.

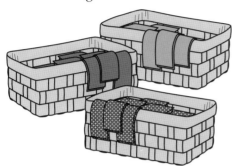

For example, when the materials list for a block pattern in this book lists seven Light Lights, you will need seven different fabrics. Do not use the same light fabric in seven places.

Construct the blocks from sets of strips sewn together. Make one strip set for each row in the block.

Arranging the Strip Sets

Fabric Value Key

■	Dark dark
▦	Light dark
▨	Dark medium
▩	Light medium
▫	Dark light
□	Light light

The following example of the seven-square block "Deseret" shows how to arrange your fabrics and construct the strip sets. The numbers (1–7) across the top of the block indicate the strip sets; each strip set reads from top to bottom. Refer to the Fabric Value Key at left to determine the value of each fabric strip that makes up the block. The letters U (up) and D (down) indicate which direction to press the seams of each strip set. Up means to press seams toward the first strip; down means to press seams away from the first strip. (See pages 22–23 for more information on pressing the strip sets.)

Press: U D U D U D U
Strip set #: 1 2 3 4 5 6 7

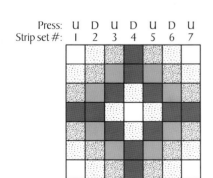

Deseret

Practice selecting and positioning values in the strip set so you will see how easy this technique is. Follow the steps below to arrange the strips into sets for the Deseret block shown below. Use the strips from your baskets.

1. Arrange the fabrics for Strip Set 1. Choose a strip from the light-light basket and place it on the table. Pick a strip of dark-light fabric and place it on top of the first strip, leaving 1½" of the first strip showing. Repeat for the remaining strips in Strip Set 1. You should have seven strips placed one on top of the other and staggered so that you can see all your choices. Repeat for each of the remaining strip sets in the block.

Strip Layout

2. Review your selections to be sure that the values are correct. Check your fabric choices with the Ruby Beholder or use one of the other value-checking ideas in "Value Vision" on page 13. Make any changes that are necessary, substituting strips of the correct value for those that look out of place. Scan each row to make certain there are no duplicate fabrics among the rows.

Be decisive. Don't spend a great deal of time deliberating over each and every strip. Trust your perceptions. One strip is not going to make or break the overall beauty of the finished quilt. It is the abundance of values, prints, and colors, strategically positioned together, that create the remarkable charm of a watercolor quilt.

If you are not going to sew the strips together now, stack each row of strips in order from the top down, label it, and put a rubber band around the stack to keep the strips in order.

Assembling the Strip Sets

When you are ready to sew the strips together in sets, first make sure that your ¼"-wide seam allowance is accurate. If you are unsure of how to do this, refer to "Sewing Guidelines" below.

1. Mark the first strip of each set with a small safety pin so that you can easily determine the correct order of subsequent strips. Leave this pin in, even while pressing.

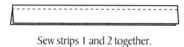

Small safety pin ——→   Strip 1

                             Strip 2

2. Sew the first and second strip together along the long edge.

Sew strips 1 and 2 together.

> *Tip* PIN A LABEL IDENTIFYING THE ROW number to the top of each sewn strip set as a reminder. It is essential to be able to arrange the strip sets in the proper order before you cut them.
>
>
>
> Strip Set 1

3. Continue sewing strips to the right edge of the strip set in the proper order.
4. Press the stitched layers together from the wrong side of the fabric to set the stitches in the seam line. Then press the seams to one direction from the right side. Press carefully to avoid pleats on the right side.

5. Press all the finished sets at once. Press all the seams of a particular strip set in the same direction, as indicated by "U" or "D" in the block diagram for the quilt you are making. (See page 21.)

Set the seams on the wrong side of the fabric.

Press the seams to one side from the right side of fabric.

> *Tip* PRESS THE COMPLETED STRIP SET rather than pairs of strips or partial sets to reduce the possibility of sewing the strips out of order.

Sewing Guidelines

Maintain consistent ¼"-wide seam allowances throughout the quilt top. This is particularly important because some of the blocks rotate within the quilt, resulting in the crosswise grain of the fabric being placed next to the lengthwise grain in neighboring blocks. There is no give in the lengthwise grain, but there is in the crosswise grain, so if your seams are not accurate, you will not be able to ease or stretch the outside edges of the blocks so that they match at the seam intersections.

Use a ¼"-wide foot on your sewing machine if one is available, move the needle position, or use the tape method that follows to sew an accurate ¼"-wide seam allowance.

1. Cut a piece of ¼" graph paper 2½" x 5". Place the paper under the presser foot, lower the foot, and insert the needle just to the right of the first line on the right edge of the paper. Make sure the paper is straight and not at an angle.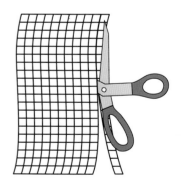

2. Position a piece of masking tape along the right edge of the paper in front of the feed dogs. Do not put tape over the feed dogs. Extend the tape about 2" beyond the back of the foot to help keep the fabric straight throughout the sewing process.

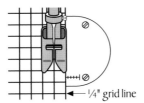

Use ¼" graph paper to position seam guide.

3. Build a four- to five-layer wall of tape so that the right edge of the fabric can ride against it as you stitch. Or use a commercial seam guide, moleskin, or Sew Perfect for the guide. Whichever method you use, always check the accuracy of your seam allowance.

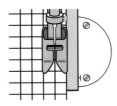

Put masking tape along the edge of the paper to guide fabric. Extend tape behind the needle for 2".

Tip

To check the accuracy of your seam allowance, cut 3 strips, each 2" x 6". Sew them together, using the ¼"-wide seam allowance you have marked or the seam guide of your choice. Press seams to one side. Measure the resulting strip set. It should be exactly 5" wide. If it is not, experiment with different seam-allowance markings. Test again and repeat until your strip set is 5" wide.

5"

Pressing Tips

- Careful steam pressing, rather than ironing, does not distort fabric, but you must be careful not to pull on the fabric. Bowed or distorted strip sets are most often the result of differences in fabric weave, quality, or weight, combined with the idiosyncrasies of your sewing machine, rather than pressing with steam.

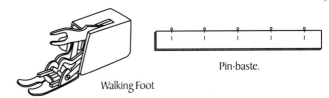

A bowed strip set is undesirable.

- If your strip sets are frequently bowed, try sewing every other strip in the opposite direction, or use a walking foot if your machine does not have a built-in, even-feed feature. If a walking foot is not available for your machine, cut all the strips exactly the same length, then pin-baste the strips about every 3" before you sew them together.

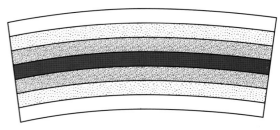

Walking Foot   Pin-baste.

Cutting the Segments for the Blocks

1. After you complete all of the strip sets for the block you are making, place Strip Set 1, *wrong side up*, on the cutting mat, with the bottom of the strip set toward you. Position Strip Set 2, *wrong side up*, on top of Strip Set 1, but offset it ¼" below the first one so that the seam allowances are not on top of each other, creating extra bulk. Stack the strip sets for each row of the block in order, with the first set on the bottom and the last set on top. This is your sewing order.

Caution: It is imperative that all the seam lines are parallel for this method of cutting. Take extra care to see that the seam lines remain parallel for the entire length of the strip sets.

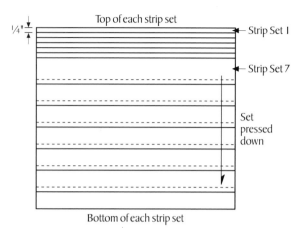

Stagger the strip sets ¼" and position them *wrong side up*, with the first set on the bottom and the last set on the top.

2. Align the rulers as you did to cut strips, then make a clean cut along the edges of the strip sets so that they are even as described on page 20. Cut 2"-wide segments from the stacked strip sets. Cutting several layers of strip sets may be a little intimidating at first, but if your rotary-cutter blade is sharp, there should be no problem. If you choose to cut multiple layers of strip units, remember to place a folded piece of fabric under the opposite edge of the ruler so the ruler will be on an even plane (page 20).

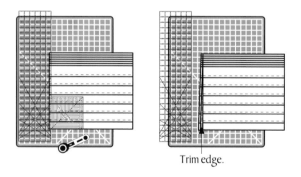

Trim edge.

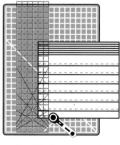

Cut 2"-wide segments.

3. Immediately after you cut each 2" segment from the stack of strip units, pin the layers together with a safety pin. Insert the pin into the wrong side of the top square of the segment that is on top of the stack. Push it through all of the rows. Each closed pin will contain all the strips, in their proper order, that are necessary to make one complete design block.

4. Check the edge of the strip set after every three to four strips to be sure that you are still making 90° cuts. Align a horizontal line of the ruler with any internal seam and make additional clean cuts as needed.

Assembling the Blocks

1. Turn the first group of fabric strips so that they are right side up, and open the safety pin. The segments should be in the proper sewing order. The first segment that you remove from the pin is the first row of the block, the second segment is the second row, continuing to the last segment.

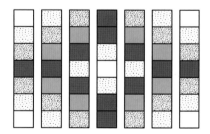

2. Sew the rows together, matching the seam intersections carefully. Pin them if necessary. If you followed the pressing plan for each strip set, opposing seams will nest together.

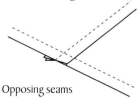

Opposing seams

3. Mark the top square of the first row with a safety pin to keep from inadvertently sewing the next segment to the wrong edge of the previous one.

4. To prevent bowed blocks, sew alternating rows in opposite directions. Do not press the seams between the rows (vertical seams) yet.

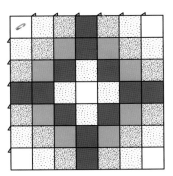

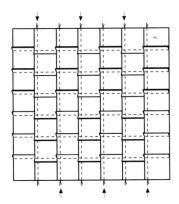

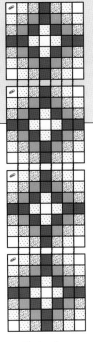

Chain-piece
when possible.

> **Tip**
>
> CHAIN-PIECE WHEREVER possible. I sew segments for four blocks at a time. When they are complete, cut the thread chains between the blocks.

5. Each quilt plan has a dot in each of the squares that identifies the top left corner of the block. Once the blocks are completed, arrange them on the design surface in the order indicated by the marked corners and the block number on the diagram.

6. Press the vertical seams in each block all in one direction; then press the vertical seams of the adjacent blocks in the opposite direction wherever possible. Because of the way that the blocks may rotate within the quilt design, some connecting blocks may have seam allowances pressed in the same direction. While this is not ideal and it stretches the rules, it is unavoidable in some circumstances. Unless those circumstances are the ones that jeopardize your salvation, you know what they say about rules. I do not twist the seam allowances to make them nest properly; I prefer to live with the bulk.

You may reposition your layout wrong side out to coordinate all the rows. Remember that all the seams in each row and block interact with the row above and below.

Some of the blocks are symmetrical, making it possible to rotate them and still maintain the same design effect. If opposing seams of adjacent, symmetrical blocks are not facing in opposite directions, try to rotate the block so that the seams lie in opposite directions.

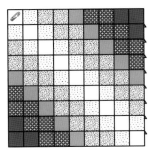 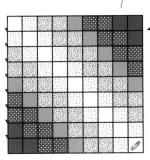

Rotate block to make seam allowances fit together.

THE QUILT PLANS

Construct all of the design blocks for the quilts according to the directions for "Making a Strip-Pieced Watercolor Quilt" on pages 19–25.

Some design blocks are used more than once in the following quilt plans. Plan ahead and save time by making enough blocks for two different quilts that use the same design blocks.

If you have extra pinned segments from a group of strip sets, make the extra blocks and set them aside. Several quilts require only one block of a certain pattern. You may find that your extra block is just exactly what you need for your next quilt. You can also sandwich and quilt a single block to make a small wall quilt.

For quilts made with more than one design block, you may choose to use a different selection of fabrics for each of the blocks. For example, "Valerry" (page 27) is made with three design blocks. Each block requires eighty-one different fabrics; when

you use a different group of fabrics for each design block, you will be able to choose a total of 243 different fabrics. If you choose to use different fabrics, do the fabric layouts for all the blocks at the same time to prevent duplications. However, it is also acceptable to duplicate fabrics from design block to design block.

Use the Fabric Value Key and fabric requirement chart accompanying each block pattern to determine the number of strips and the placement of each value.

The number of fabrics and the number of individual block patterns used in a particular quilt determine the skill level. For instance, a quilt that is made from two different Twelve-Square blocks will be more challenging than a quilt made from a single Ten-Square block pattern.

General finishing directions for all of the quilts are in "Finishing Up" on pages 97–106. The finished quilt sizes include borders if there are any.

Tic Tac Toe *by Carol Deal. This is one of a pair of quilts made from identical blocks but arranged differently. See "Who Knows?" (page 73).*

 ALERRY

by Deanna Spingola, 1994, Woodridge, Illinois, 62" x 62". The quilting and the selection of prints give this quilt a delicate, romantic look. The quilting lines accentuate the block arrangement.

FINISHED QUILT SIZE: 62" x 62" ❖ BLOCK SIZE: 13½"
BLOCKS: Nine Square One, Dark Line, Light Line ❖ SKILL LEVEL: Intermediate

Materials

DESIGN BLOCK	NINE SQUARE ONE	DARK LINE	LIGHT LINE
Strip Size	2" x 11"	2" x 20"	2" x 11"
	NO. OF STRIPS		
Dark Dark	10	9	6
Light Dark	11	16	14
Dark Medium	15	14	10
Light Medium	24	22	26
Dark Light	11	14	16
Light Light	10	6	9

44"-WIDE FABRIC

- ⅓ yd. for inner border
- ⅝ yd. for outer border
- 3½ yds. for backing
- ½ yd. for binding
- 68" x 68" piece of batting

Strip Sets

Refer to "Making a Strip-Pieced Watercolor Quilt" on pages 19–25 for information on cutting and assembling strip sets and blocks.

Combine three different blocks to make this quilt. You may use 243 different fabrics or just 81, duplicating the prints from design block to design block. If you prefer, just duplicate your favorites.

Arrange the strips as shown below and sew them together. Make 1 of each strip set for each design block; label.

Nine Square One Blocks

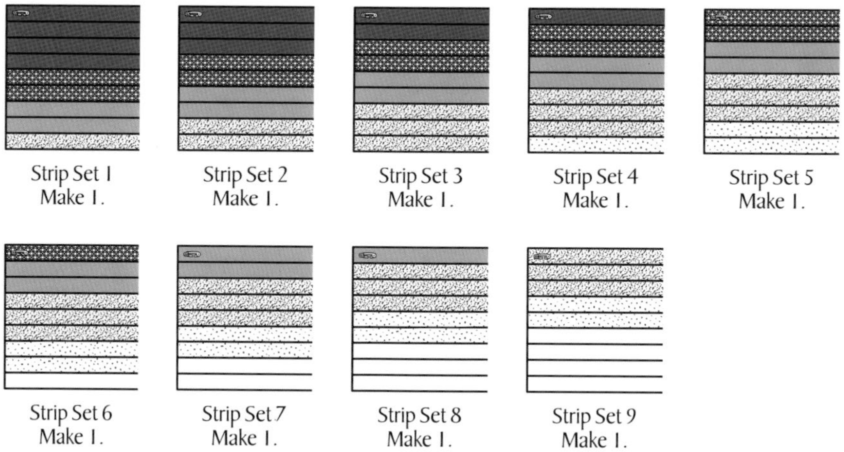

Strip Set 1
Make 1.

Strip Set 2
Make 1.

Strip Set 3
Make 1.

Strip Set 4
Make 1.

Strip Set 5
Make 1.

Strip Set 6
Make 1.

Strip Set 7
Make 1.

Strip Set 8
Make 1.

Strip Set 9
Make 1.

Dark Line Blocks

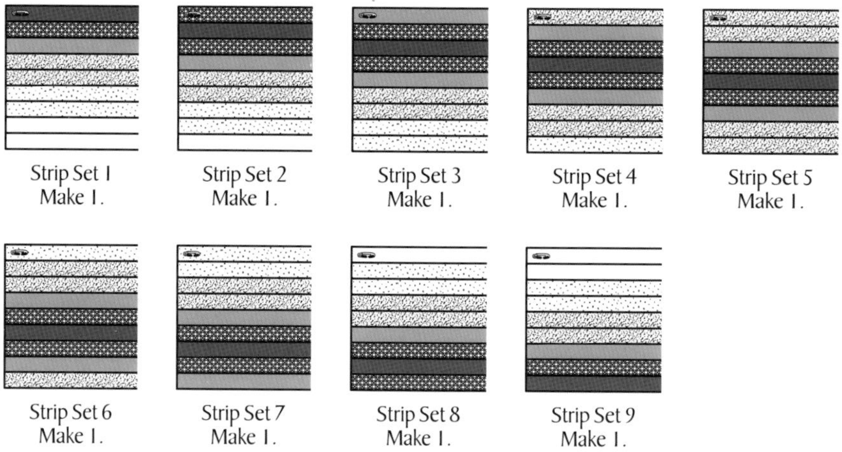

Strip Set 1
Make 1.

Strip Set 2
Make 1.

Strip Set 3
Make 1.

Strip Set 4
Make 1.

Strip Set 5
Make 1.

Strip Set 6
Make 1.

Strip Set 7
Make 1.

Strip Set 8
Make 1.

Strip Set 9
Make 1.

Light Line Blocks

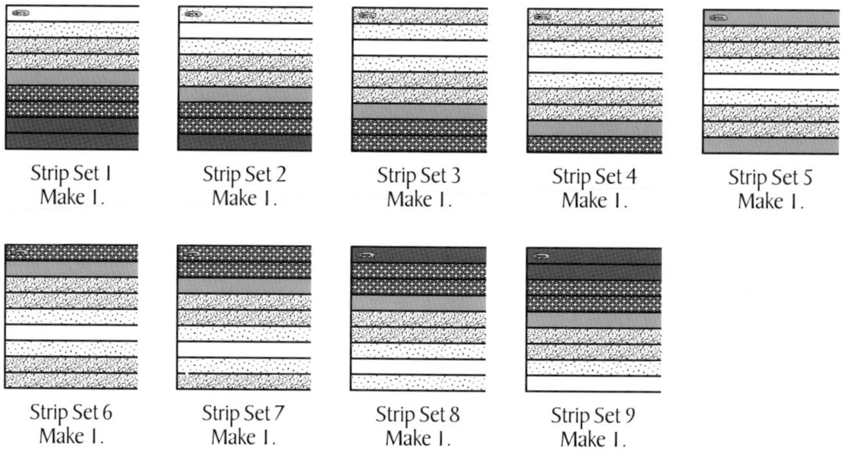

Strip Set 1
Make 1.

Strip Set 2
Make 1.

Strip Set 3
Make 1.

Strip Set 4
Make 1.

Strip Set 5
Make 1.

Strip Set 6
Make 1.

Strip Set 7
Make 1.

Strip Set 8
Make 1.

Strip Set 9
Make 1.

Block Construction

Stack the strip sets for the Nine Square One blocks in the proper order as described on pages 23–24 and crosscut them into 4 segments, each 2" wide. Stack and cut 8 segments for the Dark Line blocks, and 4 segments for the Light Line blocks. Sew the segments together to make 4 Nine Square One blocks, 8 Dark Line blocks, and 4 Light Line blocks.

Press: U D U D U D U D U
Strip set #: 1 2 3 4 5 6 7 8 9

Block 1
Nine Square One
Make 4.

Press: U D U D U D U D U
Strip set #: 1 2 3 4 5 6 7 8 9

Block 2
Dark Line
Make 8.

Press: U D U D U D U D U
Strip set #: 1 2 3 4 5 6 7 8 9

Block 3
Light Line
Make 4.

Quilt Top Assembly

1. Arrange the blocks in 4 rows of 4 blocks each, referring to the quilt plan below and rotating the blocks as necessary. Sew the blocks together as directed in "Assembling the Quilt Top" on page 97.

3	2	2	3
2	1	1	2
2	1	1	2
3	2	2	3

Dots on the quilt plan indicate the upper left corner of the design block.

2. From the inner border fabric, cut 6 strips, each 1¾" x 42". Cut 6 strips, each 3" x 42", from outer border fabric.
3. Sew each inner border strip to an outer border strip. Press the seam toward the outer border strip. Cut 2 strips in half crosswise. Sew 1 strip to each of the remaining strips, using a diagonal seam as shown on pages 97–98.
4. Measure the quilt top for borders as described in "Making Borders with Mitered Corners" on page 98. Cut the border strips to fit and stitch them to the quilt top, mitering the corners.
5. Layer the quilt top with backing and batting; baste. Quilt as desired.
6. From binding fabric, cut 6 strips, each 2½" x 42". Sew them together with a diagonal seam (page 105) to make one piece of binding that is long enough for the quilt. Bind the edges of the quilt.

$\mathscr{S}$PINGOLA SPIN

by Deanna Spingola, 1994, Woodridge, Illinois, 66½" x 66½".
Motion and commotion are the focus and design of this quilt.

FINISHED QUILT SIZE: 66½" x 66½" ❖ BLOCK SIZE: 15"
BLOCKS: Dark Arrow, Midnight, Toltec ❖ SKILL LEVEL: Advanced

Materials

DESIGN BLOCK	DARK ARROW	MIDNIGHT	TOLTEC
Strip Size	2" x 11"	2" x 11"	2" x 20"
	NO. OF STRIPS		
Dark Dark	20	20	20
Light Dark	16	19	16
Dark Medium	16	18	16
Light Medium	16	17	16
Dark Light	16	14	16
Light Light	16	12	16

44"-WIDE FABRIC

- ⅞ yd. for border
- 4 yds. for backing
- ⅔ yd. for binding
- 72" x 72" piece of batting

Strip Sets

Refer to "Making a Strip-Pieced Watercolor Quilt" on pages 19–25 for information on cutting and assembling strip sets and blocks.

Arrange the strips as shown below and sew them together. Make 1 of each strip set for each design block; label.

Dark Arrow Blocks

Strip Set 1 — Make 1.
Strip Set 2 — Make 1.
Strip Set 3 — Make 1.
Strip Set 4 — Make 1.
Strip Set 5 — Make 1.

Strip Set 6 — Make 1.
Strip Set 7 — Make 1.
Strip Set 8 — Make 1.
Strip Set 9 — Make 1.
Strip Set 10 — Make 1.

Midnight Blocks

Strip Set 1 — Make 1.
Strip Set 2 — Make 1.
Strip Set 3 — Make 1.
Strip Set 4 — Make 1.
Strip Set 5 — Make 1.

Strip Set 6 — Make 1.
Strip Set 7 — Make 1.
Strip Set 8 — Make 1.
Strip Set 9 — Make 1.
Strip Set 10 — Make 1.

Toltec Blocks

Strip Set 1 — Make 1.
Strip Set 2 — Make 1.
Strip Set 3 — Make 1.
Strip Set 4 — Make 1.
Strip Set 5 — Make 1.

Strip Set 6 — Make 1.
Strip Set 7 — Make 1.
Strip Set 8 — Make 1.
Strip Set 9 — Make 1.
Strip Set 10 — Make 1.

Block Construction

Stack the strip sets for the Dark Arrow blocks in the proper order as described on pages 23–24 and crosscut them into 4 segments, each 2" wide. Repeat with the strip sets for the Midnight block. Stack and cut 8 segments for the Toltec block. Sew them together to make 4 Dark Arrow blocks, 4 Midnight blocks, and 8 Toltec blocks.

Press: U D U D U D U D U D
Strip set #: 1 2 3 4 5 6 7 8 9 10

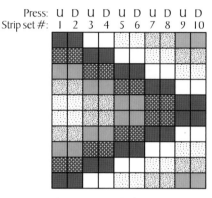

Block 1
Dark Arrow
Make 4.

Press: U D U D U D U D U D
Strip set #: 1 2 3 4 5 6 7 8 9 10

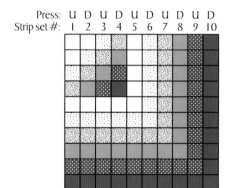

Block 2
Midnight
Make 4.

Press: U D U D U D U D U D
Strip set #: 1 2 3 4 5 6 7 8 9 10

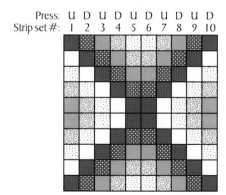

Block 3
Toltec
Make 8.

Quilt Top Assembly

1. Arrange the blocks in 4 rows of 4 blocks each, referring to the quilt plan below. Rotate and alternate the blocks as necessary. Sew the blocks together as directed in "Assembling the Quilt Top" on page 97.

2 •	• 3	• 3	• 2
3 •	• 1	1 •	• 3
3 •	• 1	1 •	• 3
2 •	• 3	3 •	• 2

Dots on the quilt plan indicate the upper left corner of the design block.

2. From border fabric, cut 8 strips, each 3½" x 42". Sew strips together in pairs, end to end, using a diagonal seam as shown on pages 97–98.
3. Measure the quilt top for borders as described in "Making Borders with Mitered Corners" on page 98. Cut the border strips to fit and stitch them to the quilt top, mitering the corners.
4. Layer the quilt top with backing and batting; baste. Quilt as desired.
5. From binding fabric, cut 7 strips, each 2½" x 42". Sew them together with a diagonal seam (page 105) to make one piece of binding that is long enough for the quilt. Bind the edges of the quilt.

Somewhere in Time

by Deanna Spingola, 1994, Woodridge, Illinois, 51½" x 51½". Value creates depth in the funnel shapes. Temporarily lose yourself as you embark on a visual journey.

FINISHED QUILT SIZE: 51½" x 51½" ❖ BLOCK SIZE: 15"

BLOCKS: Dark Arrow, Midnight, Toltec ❖ SKILL LEVEL: Intermediate

Materials

DESIGN BLOCK	DARK ARROW	MIDNIGHT	TOLTEC
Strip Size	2" x 11"	2" x 11"	2" x 2"
	NO. OF STRIPS		
Dark Dark	20	20	20
Light Dark	16	19	16
Dark Medium	16	18	16
Light Medium	16	17	16
Dark Light	16	14	16
Light Light	16	12	16

44"-WIDE FABRIC

- ¾ yd. for border
- 3¼ yds. for backing
- ½ yd. for binding
- 57" x 57" piece of batting

Strip Sets

Refer to "Making a Strip-Pieced Watercolor Quilt" on pages 19–25 for information on cutting and assembling strip sets and blocks.

Arrange the strips as shown below and sew them together. Make 1 of each strip set for each design block; label.

Dark Arrow Blocks

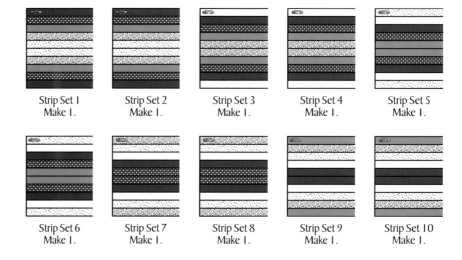

Midnight Blocks

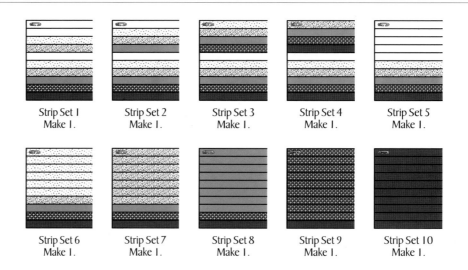

Block Construction

Stack the strip sets for the Dark Arrow block in the proper order as described on pages 23–24 and crosscut them into 4 segments, each 2" wide. Repeat with the strip sets for the Midnight blocks. Sew the segments together to make 4 Dark Arrow and 4 Midnight blocks. Sew squares together to make 1 Toltec block.

Press: U D U D U D U D U D
Strip set #: 1 2 3 4 5 6 7 8 9 10

Block 1
Dark Arrow
Make 4.

Press: U D U D U D U D U D
Strip set #: 1 2 3 4 5 6 7 8 9 10

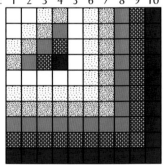

Block 2
Midnight
Make 4.

Press: U D U D U D U D U D
Strip set #: 1 2 3 4 5 6 7 8 9 10

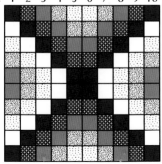

Block 3
Toltec
Make 1.

Quilt Top Assembly

1. Arrange the blocks in 3 rows of 3 blocks each, referring to the quilt plan below. Alternate and rotate the blocks as necessary. Sew the blocks together as directed in "Assembling the Quilt Top" on page 97.

2	1	2
1	3	1
2	1	2

Dots on the quilt plan indicate the upper left corner of the design block.

2. From border fabric, cut 6 strips, each 3½" x 42".
3. Cut 2 strips in half crosswise. Sew 1 strip to each of the remaining strips, using a diagonal seam as shown on pages 97–98.
4. Measure the quilt top for borders as described in "Making Borders with Mitered Corners" on page 98. Cut the border strips to fit and stitch them to the quilt top, mitering the corners.
5. Layer the quilt top with backing and batting; baste. Quilt as desired.
6. From binding fabric, cut 6 strips, each 2½" x 42". Sew them together with a diagonal seam (page 105) to make one piece of binding that is long enough for the quilt. Bind the edges of the quilt.

$\mathscr{S}$CENIC CROSSROADS

by Denise Griffin, 1994, Downers Grove, Illinois, 67½" x 67½".
This quilt uses two design blocks. It is beautifully hand quilted.

FINISHED QUILT SIZE: 67½" x 67½" ❖ BLOCK SIZE: 15"
BLOCKS: Cartwheel, Toltec ❖ SKILL LEVEL: Intermediate

Materials

DESIGN BLOCK		CARTWHEEL	TOLTEC
Strip Size		2" x 20"	2" x 20"
		NO. OF STRIPS	
	Dark Dark	28	20
	Light Dark	13	16
	Dark Medium	15	16
	Light Medium	16	16
	Dark Light	13	16
	Light Light	15	16

44"-WIDE FABRIC

- ½ yd. for inner border
- ¾ yd. for outer border
- 4⅛ yds. for backing
- ⅔ yd. for binding
- 73" x 73" piece of batting

Strip Sets

Refer to "Making a Strip-Pieced Watercolor Quilt" on pages 19–25 for information on cutting and assembling strip sets and blocks.

Arrange the strips as shown below and sew them together. Make 1 of each strip set for each design block; label.

Cartwheel Blocks

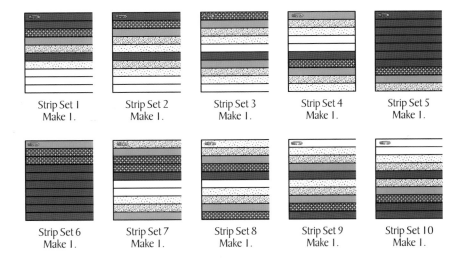

Strip Set 1
Make 1.

Strip Set 2
Make 1.

Strip Set 3
Make 1.

Strip Set 4
Make 1.

Strip Set 5
Make 1.

Strip Set 6
Make 1.

Strip Set 7
Make 1.

Strip Set 8
Make 1.

Strip Set 9
Make 1.

Strip Set 10
Make 1.

Toltec Blocks

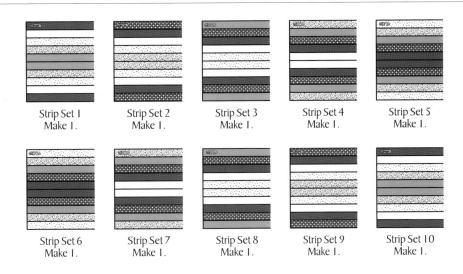

Strip Set 1
Make 1.

Strip Set 2
Make 1.

Strip Set 3
Make 1.

Strip Set 4
Make 1.

Strip Set 5
Make 1.

Strip Set 6
Make 1.

Strip Set 7
Make 1.

Strip Set 8
Make 1.

Strip Set 9
Make 1.

Strip Set 10
Make 1.

Block Construction

Stack the strip sets for the Cartwheel block in the proper order as described on pages 23–24 and crosscut them into 8 segments, each 2" wide. Repeat with the strip sets for the Toltec block. Sew the segments together to make 8 Cartwheel blocks and 8 Toltec blocks.

Press: U D U D U D U D U D
Strip set #: 1 2 3 4 5 6 7 8 9 10

Block 1
Cartwheel
Make 8.

Press: U D U D U D U D U D
Strip set #: 1 2 3 4 5 6 7 8 9 10

Block 2
Toltec
Make 8.

Quilt Top Assembly

1. Arrange the blocks in 4 rows of 4 blocks each, referring to the quilt plan below. Sew the blocks together as directed in "Assembling the Quilt Top" on page 97.

2	1	2	1
1	2	1	2
2	1	2	1
1	2	1	2

Dots on the quilt plan indicate the upper left corner of the design block.

2. From the inner border fabric, cut 8 strips, each 1½" x 42". Cut 8 strips, each 3" x 42", from outer border fabric.
3. Sew each inner border strip to an outer border strip. Press the seam toward the outer border strip. Sew pairs of border strips together, using a diagonal seam as shown on pages 97–98. Make 4 border strips.
4. Measure the quilt top for borders as described in "Making Borders with Mitered Corners" on page 98. Cut the border strips to fit and stitch them to the quilt top, mitering the corners.
5. Layer the quilt top with backing and batting; baste. Quilt as desired.
6. From binding fabric, cut 8 strips, each 2½" x 42". Sew them together with a diagonal seam (page 105) to make one piece of binding that is long enough for the quilt. Bind the edges of the quilt.

$\mathcal{S}$TARGAZER

by Patricia McCormack, 1994, Downers Grove, Illinois, 53½" x 53½". Light and dark values in cool and warm colors combine in this quilt, which is framed by a midnight jewel border highlighted by stars. This hand-quilted lap quilt is dedicated to Mary and Melvin Genaze, Pattie's parents. Her mother taught her to quilt, and her talented father drew the quilt design.

FINISHED QUILT SIZE: 53½" x 53½" ❖ BLOCK SIZE: 15"
BLOCKS: Light Arrow, Toltec ❖ SKILL LEVEL: Intermediate

Materials

DESIGN BLOCK	LIGHT ARROW	TOLTEC
Strip Size	2" x 16"	2" x 11"
	NO. OF STRIPS	
Dark Dark	16	20
Light Dark	16	16
Dark Medium	16	16
Light Medium	16	16
Dark Light	16	16
Light Light	20	16

44"-WIDE FABRIC

- ⅓ yd. for inner border
- ⅝ yd. for outer border
- ¼ yd. total assorted yellow fabrics for outer border
- 3¼ yds. for backing
- ½ yd. for binding
- 58" x 58" piece of batting

Strip Sets

Refer to "Making a Strip-Pieced Watercolor Quilt" on pages 19–25 for information on cutting and assembling strip sets and blocks.

Arrange the strips as shown below and sew them together. Make 1 of each strip set for each design block; label.

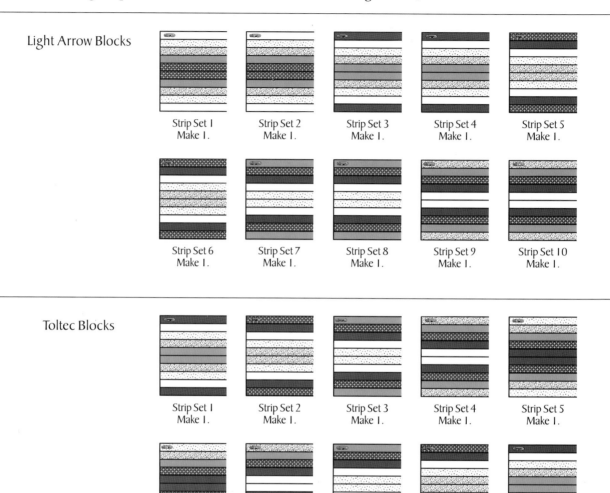

Light Arrow Blocks

Strip Set 1
Make 1.

Strip Set 2
Make 1.

Strip Set 3
Make 1.

Strip Set 4
Make 1.

Strip Set 5
Make 1.

Strip Set 6
Make 1.

Strip Set 7
Make 1.

Strip Set 8
Make 1.

Strip Set 9
Make 1.

Strip Set 10
Make 1.

Toltec Blocks

Strip Set 1
Make 1.

Strip Set 2
Make 1.

Strip Set 3
Make 1.

Strip Set 4
Make 1.

Strip Set 5
Make 1.

Strip Set 6
Make 1.

Strip Set 7
Make 1.

Strip Set 8
Make 1.

Strip Set 9
Make 1.

Strip Set 10
Make 1.

Block Construction

Stack the strip sets for the Light Arrow blocks in the proper order as described on pages 23–24 and crosscut them into 6 segments, each 2" wide. Stack and cut 3 segments, each 2" wide, for the Toltec block. Sew the segments together to make 6 Light Arrow blocks and 3 Toltec blocks.

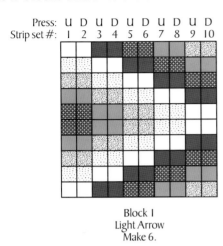

Press: U D U D U D U D U D
Strip set #: 1 2 3 4 5 6 7 8 9 10

Block 1
Light Arrow
Make 6.

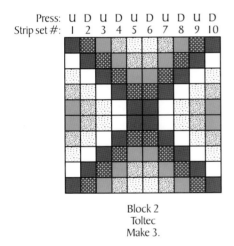

Press: U D U D U D U D U D
Strip set #: 1 2 3 4 5 6 7 8 9 10

Block 2
Toltec
Make 3.

Quilt Top Assembly

1. Arrange the blocks in 3 rows of 3 blocks each, referring to the quilt plan below. Alternate and rotate the blocks as necessary. Sew the blocks together as directed in "Assembling the Quilt Top" on page 97.

Dots on the quilt plan indicate the upper left corner of the design block.

2. From the inner border fabric, cut 6 strips, each 1½" x 42".
3. From the outer border fabric, cut:
   7 strips, each 3½" wide; crosscut into:
      8 rectangles, each 3½" x 12½"
      8 rectangles, each 3½" x 10"
   2 strips, each 1½" wide; crosscut into:
      48 squares, each 1½" x 1½"
   2 strips, each 1⅞" wide; crosscut into
      24 squares, each 1⅞" x 1⅞"; cut each square once diagonally for 48 triangles.
4. From assorted yellow fabrics, cut:
   12 squares, each 1½" x 1½"
   24 squares, each 1⅞" x 1⅞"; cut each 1⅞" square once diagonally to yield 48 triangles.
5. Sew each yellow triangle to a triangle of outer border fabric.

6. Arrange 12 star blocks as shown. Sew squares together into rows; sew the rows together.

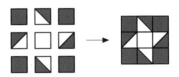

7. Sew star blocks to rectangles of outer border fabric as shown. Make 4 border strips.

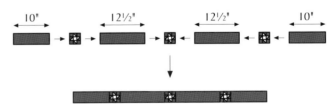

8. Cut 2 of the inner border strips in half crosswise. Sew 1 short strip to each of the remaining strips, using a diagonal seam (pages 97–98). Sew each inner border strip to a pieced outer border strip. Press the seam toward the inner border strip.
9. Measure the quilt top for borders as described in "Making Borders with Mitered Corners" on page 98. Cut the border strips to fit and stitch them to the quilt top, mitering the corners.
10. Layer the quilt top with backing and batting; baste. Quilt as desired.
11. From binding fabric, cut 6 strips, each 2½" x 42". Sew them together with a diagonal seam (page 105) to make one piece of binding that is long enough for the quilt. Bind the edges of the quilt.

COSMIC ENERGY

by Deanna Spingola, 1994, Woodridge, Illinois, 55½" x 55½". Sizzling bright red combined with orange suggests motion.

FINISHED QUILT SIZE: 55½" x 55½" ◈ BLOCK SIZE: 12"
BLOCKS: Mediator, Corner Lot, Positive/Negative ◈ SKILL LEVEL: Advanced

Materials

DESIGN BLOCK	MEDIATOR	CORNER LOT	POSITIVE/ NEGATIVE
Strip Size	2" x 11"	2" x 11"	2" x 20"
	NO. OF STRIPS		
Dark Dark	8	9	7
Light Dark	10	13	12
Dark Medium	14	16	12
Light Medium	14	8	12
Dark Light	10	13	13
Light Light	8	5	8

44"-WIDE FABRIC

- ⅓ yd. for inner border
- ⅝ yd. for outer border
- 3½ yds. for backing
- ½ yd. for binding
- 61" x 61" piece of batting

Strip Sets

Refer to "Making a Strip-Pieced Watercolor Quilt" on pages 19–25 for information on cutting and assembling strip sets and blocks.

Arrange the strips as shown below and sew them together. Make 1 of each strip set for each design block; label.

Mediator Blocks

Strip Set 1
Make 1.

Strip Set 2
Make 1.

Strip Set 3
Make 1.

Strip Set 4
Make 1.

Strip Set 5
Make 1.

Strip Set 6
Make 1.

Strip Set 7
Make 1.

Strip Set 8
Make 1.

Corner Lot Blocks

Strip Set 1
Make 1.

Strip Set 2
Make 1.

Strip Set 3
Make 1.

Strip Set 4
Make 1.

Strip Set 5
Make 1.

Strip Set 6
Make 1.

Strip Set 7
Make 1.

Strip Set 8
Make 1.

Positive/Negative Blocks

Strip Set 1
Make 1.

Strip Set 2
Make 1.

Strip Set 3
Make 1.

Strip Set 4
Make 1.

Strip Set 5
Make 1.

Strip Set 6
Make 1.

Strip Set 7
Make 1.

Strip Set 8
Make 1.

Block Construction

Stack the strip sets for the Mediator block in the proper order as described on pages 23–24 and cross-cut them into 4 segments, each 2" wide. Repeat with the Corner Lot strip sets. Stack and cut 8 segments, each 2" wide, for the Positive/Negative blocks. Sew the segments together to make 4 Mediator blocks, 4 Corner Lot blocks, and 8 Positive/Negative blocks.

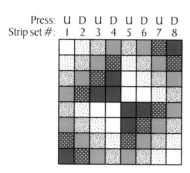

Block 1
Mediator
Make 4.

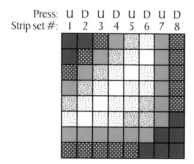

Block 2
Corner Lot
Make 4.

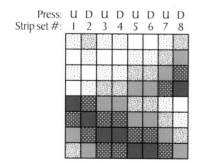

Block 3
Positive/Negative
Make 8.

Quilt Top Assembly

1. Arrange the blocks in 4 rows of 4 blocks each, referring to the quilt plan below. Alternate and rotate the blocks as necessary. Sew the blocks together as directed in "Assembling the Quilt Top" on page 97.

Dots on the quilt indicate the upper left corner of the design block.

2. From the inner border fabric, cut 6 strips, each 1½" x 42". Cut 6 strips, each 3" x 42", from outer border fabric.
3. Sew each inner border strip to an outer border strip. Press the seam toward the outer border strip. Cut 2 of the resulting border strips in half crosswise. Sew 1 short strip to each of the remaining strips, using a diagonal seam as shown on pages 97–98.
4. Measure the quilt top for borders as described in "Making Borders with Mitered Corners" on page 98. Cut the border strips to fit and stitch them to the quilt top, mitering the corners.
5. Layer the quilt top with backing and batting; baste. Quilt as desired.
6. From binding fabric, cut 6 strips, each 2½" x 42". Sew them together with a diagonal seam (page 105) to make one piece of binding that is long enough for the quilt. Bind the edges of the quilt.

$\mathcal{M}$ELANIE'S WIND CHIMES

by Deanna Spingola, 1994, Woodridge, Illinois, 55½" x 55½". Enjoy the harmony the warm and cool colors create. A combination of quilting techniques enhances the quilt design.

FINISHED QUILT SIZE: 55½" x 55½" ❖ BLOCK SIZE: 12"
BLOCKS: Corner Lot, Mediator, Goodness ❖ SKILL LEVEL: Intermediate

Materials

DESIGN BLOCK		CORNER LOT	MEDIATOR	GOODNESS
Strip Size		2" x 11"	2" x 11"	2" x 20"
		NO. OF STRIPS		
	Dark Dark	9	8	11
	Light Dark	13	10	11
	Dark Medium	16	14	12
	Light Medium	8	14	11
	Dark Light	13	10	10
	Light Light	5	8	9

44"-WIDE FABRIC

- ¾ yd. for border
- 3½ yds. for backing
- ½ yd. for binding
- 61" x 61" piece of batting

Strip Sets

Refer to "Making a Strip-Pieced Watercolor Quilt" on pages 19–25 for information on cutting and assembling strip sets and blocks.

Arrange the strips as shown below and sew them together. Make 1 of each strip set for each design block; label.

Corner Lot Blocks

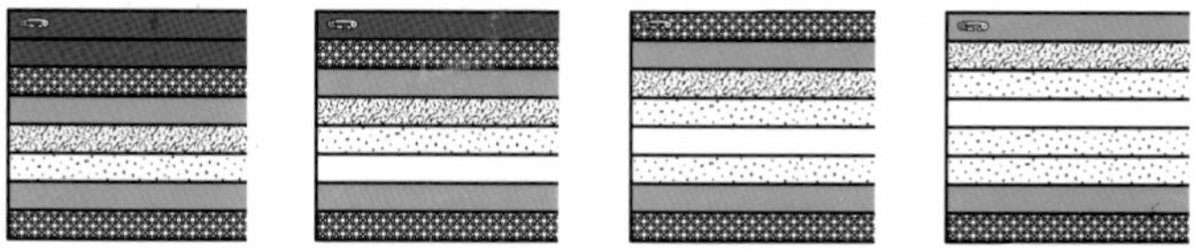

Strip Set 1
Make 1.

Strip Set 2
Make 1.

Strip Set 3
Make 1.

Strip Set 4
Make 1.

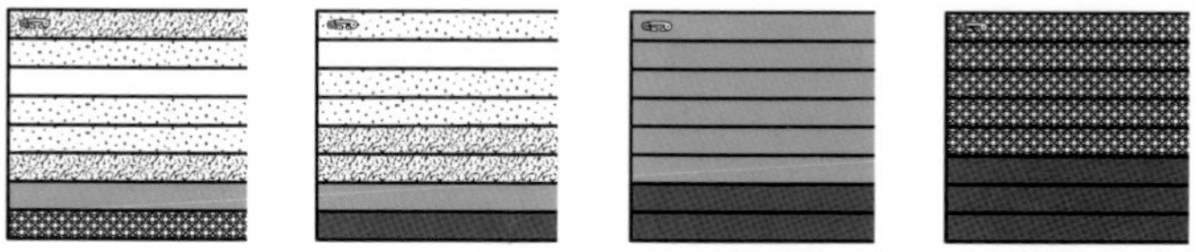

Strip Set 5
Make 1.

Strip Set 6
Make 1.

Strip Set 7
Make 1.

Strip Set 8
Make 1.

Mediator Blocks

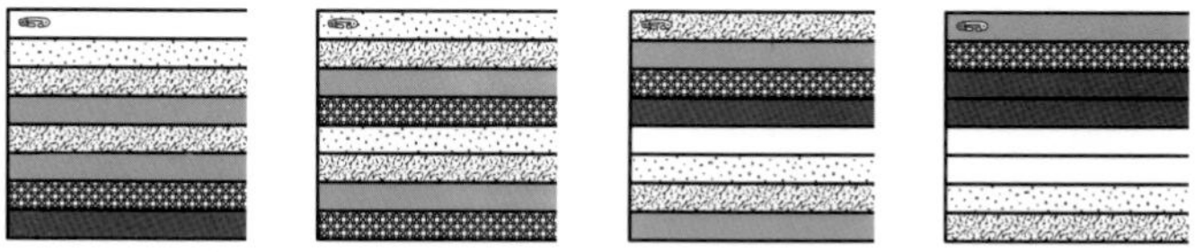

Strip Set 1
Make 1.

Strip Set 2
Make 1.

Strip Set 3
Make 1.

Strip Set 4
Make 1.

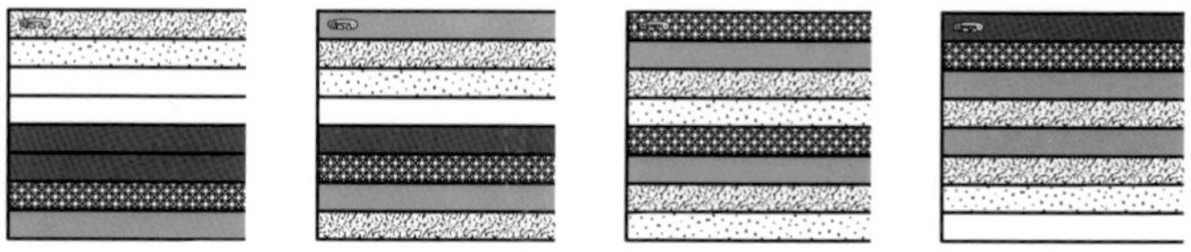

Strip Set 5
Make 1.

Strip Set 6
Make 1.

Strip Set 7
Make 1.

Strip Set 8
Make 1.

Goodness Blocks

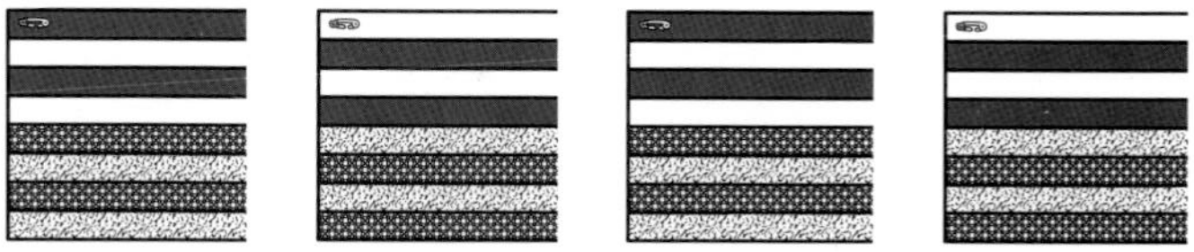

Strip Set 1
Make 1.

Strip Set 2
Make 1.

Strip Set 3
Make 1.

Strip Set 4
Make 1.

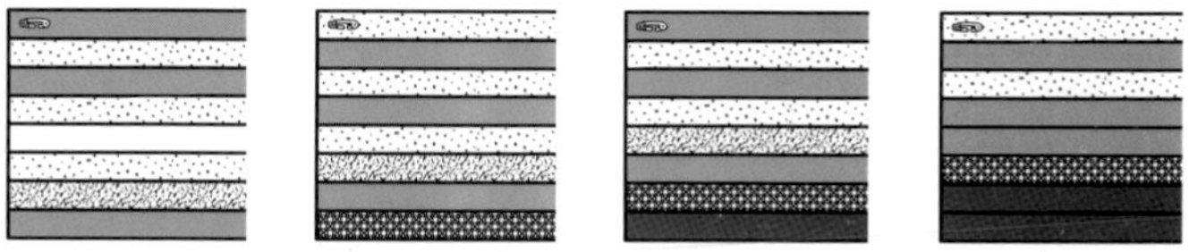

Strip Set 5
Make 1.

Strip Set 6
Make 1.

Strip Set 7
Make 1.

Strip Set 8
Make 1.

Block Construction

Stack the strip sets for the Corner Lot blocks in the proper order as described on pages 23–24 and crosscut them into 4 segments, each 2" wide. Repeat with the strip sets for the Mediator blocks. Stack and cut 8 segments, each 2" wide, for the Goodness blocks. Sew the segments together to make 4 Corner Lot blocks, 4 Mediator blocks, and 8 Goodness blocks.

Press: U D U D U D U D
Strip set #: 1 2 3 4 5 6 7 8

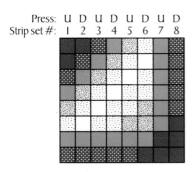

Block 1
Corner Lot
Make 4.

Press: U D U D U D U D
Strip set #: 1 2 3 4 5 6 7 8

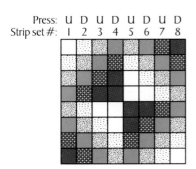

Block 2
Mediator
Make 4.

Press: U D U D U D U D
Strip set #: 1 2 3 4 5 6 7 8

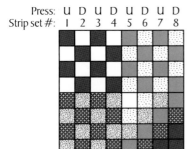

Block 3
Goodness
Make 8.

Quilt Top Assembly

1. Arrange the blocks in 4 rows of 4 blocks each, referring to the quilt plan below. Alternate and rotate the blocks as necessary. Sew the blocks together as directed in "Assembling the Quilt Top" on page 97.

Dots on the quilt plan indicate the
upper left corner of the design block.

2. From border fabric, cut 6 strips, each 4" x 42". Cut 2 strips in half crosswise and sew 1 piece to each of the remaining strips, using a diagonal seam as shown on pages 97–98.
3. Measure the quilt top for borders as described in "Making Borders with Mitered Corners" on page 98. Cut the border strips to fit and stitch them to the quilt top, mitering the corners.
4. Layer the quilt top with backing and batting; baste. Quilt as desired.
5. From binding fabric, cut 6 strips, each 2½" x 42". Sew them together with a diagonal seam (page 105) to make one piece of binding that is long enough for the quilt. Bind the edges of the quilt.

WATERCOLOR RAILS

*by Deanna Spingola, 1994, Woodridge, Illinois,
43½" x 52½". Although the layout is traditional,
the design takes on an added dimension with the
multitude of floral fabrics.*

FINISHED QUILT SIZE: 43½" x 52½" ❖ BLOCK SIZE: 9" ❖ BLOCK: Six Square One ❖ SKILL LEVEL: Beginner

Materials

2" X 42" STRIPS

■	Dark Dark	6
■	Light Dark	6
■	Dark Medium	6
■	Light Medium	6
□	Dark Light	6
□	Light Light	6

44"-WIDE FABRIC

- ⅓ yd. for inner border
- ⅝ yd. for outer border
- 3 yds. for backing
- ½ yd. for binding
- 50" x 59" piece of batting

Strip Sets

Refer to "Making a Strip-Pieced Watercolor Quilt" on pages 19–25 for information on cutting and assembling strip sets and blocks. If any of the selected strips measure less than 2" x 42", make them longer by sewing an additional strip to one end.

Arrange the strips as shown below and sew them together. Make 1 of each strip set; label.

Six Square One Blocks

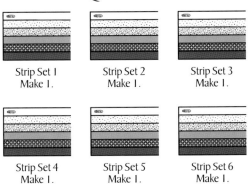

Strip Set 1
Make 1.

Strip Set 2
Make 1.

Strip Set 3
Make 1.

Strip Set 4
Make 1.

Strip Set 5
Make 1.

Strip Set 6
Make 1.

Block Construction

Stack the strip sets in the proper order as described on pages 23–24 and crosscut them into 20 segments, each 2"-wide. Sew the segments together to make 20 blocks.

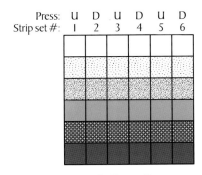

Press: U D U D U D
Strip set #: 1 2 3 4 5 6

Six Square One
Make 20.

Quilt Top Assembly

1. Arrange the blocks in 5 rows of 4 blocks each, rotating the blocks as necessary.

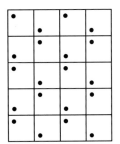

Dots on the quilt plan indicate the
upper left corner of the design block.

2. From the inner border fabric, cut 6 strips, each 1½" x 42". Cut 6 strips, each 3" x 42", from outer border fabric.

3. Sew each inner border strip to an outer border strip. Press the seam toward the outer border strip. Cut 2 of the resulting border strips in half crosswise. Sew 1 short strip to each of the remaining strips, using a diagonal seam as shown on pages 97–98.

4. Measure the quilt top for borders as described in "Making Borders with Mitered Corners" on page 98. Cut the border strips to fit and stitch them to the quilt top, mitering the corners.

5. Layer the quilt top with backing and batting; baste. Quilt as desired.

6. From binding fabric, cut 6 strips, each 2½" x 42". Sew them together with a diagonal seam (page 105) to make one piece of binding that is long enough for the quilt. Bind the edges of the quilt.

JORDAN'S FERRIS WHEEL

by Deanna Spingola, 1994, Woodridge, Illinois, 48" x 48". An impressionistic ferris wheel is surrounded with a fencelike fabric. Bright orange squares highlight the rotating cars, adding warmth to the quilt.

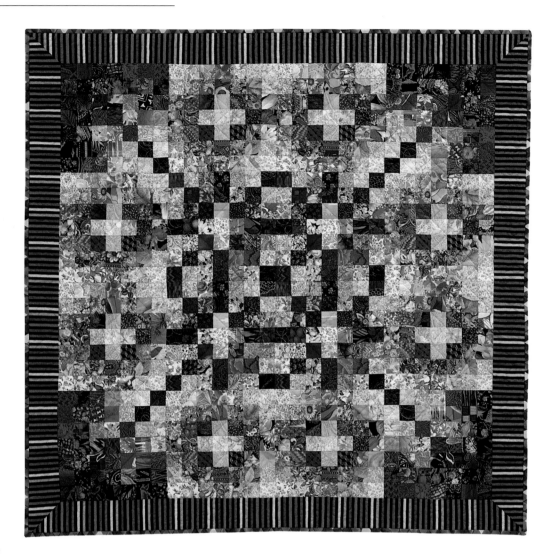

FINISHED QUILT SIZE: 48" x 48" ✧ BLOCK SIZE: 10½"
BLOCKS: Frank, Beguile, King's Crown ✧ SKILL LEVEL: Intermediate

Materials

DESIGN BLOCK	FRANK	BEGUILE	KING'S CROWN
Strip Size	2" x 11"	2" x 11"	2" x 20"
	NO. OF STRIPS		
Dark Dark	20	19	4
Light Dark	0	10	4
Dark Medium	8	8	12
Light Medium	8	6	12
Dark Light	12	4	12
Light Light	1	2	5

44"-WIDE FABRIC

- ⅝ yd. for border
- 3 yds. for backing
- ½ yd. for binding
- 54" x 54" piece of batting

Strip Sets

Refer to "Making a Strip-Pieced Watercolor Quilt" on pages 19–25 for information on cutting and assembling strip sets and blocks.

Arrange the strips as shown below and sew them together. Make 1 of each strip set for each design block; label.

Frank Blocks

Strip Set 1
Make 1.

Strip Set 2
Make 1.

Strip Set 3
Make 1.

Strip Set 4
Make 1.

Strip Set 5
Make 1.

Strip Set 6
Make 1.

Strip Set 7
Make 1.

Beguile Blocks

Strip Set 1
Make 1.

Strip Set 2
Make 1.

Strip Set 3
Make 1.

Strip Set 4
Make 1.

Strip Set 5
Make 1.

Strip Set 6
Make 1.

Strip Set 7
Make 1.

King's Crown Blocks

Strip Set 1
Make 1.

Strip Set 2
Make 1.

Strip Set 3
Make 1.

Strip Set 4
Make 1.

Strip Set 5
Make 1.

Strip Set 6
Make 1.

Strip Set 7
Make 1.

Block Construction

Stack the strip sets for the Frank blocks in the proper order as described on pages 23–24 and cross-cut them into 4 segments, each 2" wide. Repeat with the strip sets for the Beguile blocks. Stack and cut 8 segments for the King's Crown blocks. Sew them together to make 4 Frank blocks, 4 Beguile blocks, and 8 King's Crown blocks.

Press: U D U D U D U
Strip set #: 1 2 3 4 5 6 7

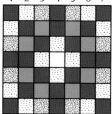

Block 1
Frank
Make 4.

Press: U D U D U D U
Strip set #: 1 2 3 4 5 6 7

Block 2
Beguile
Make 4.

Press: U D U D U D U
Strip set #: 1 2 3 4 5 6 7

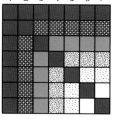

Block 3
King's Crown
Make 8.

Quilt Top Assembly

1. Arrange the blocks in 4 rows of 4 blocks each, referring to the quilt plan below. Alternate and rotate the blocks as necessary. Sew the blocks together as directed in "Assembling the Quilt Top" on page 97.

2	3	3	2
3	1	1	3
3	1	1	3
2	3	3	2

Dots on the quilt plan indicate the upper left corner of the design block.

2. From border fabric, cut 6 strips, each 3¼ x 42".
3. Cut 2 border strips in half crosswise. Sew 1 strip to each of the remaining strips, using a diagonal seam as shown on pages 97–98.
4. Measure the quilt top for borders as described in "Making Borders with Mitered Corners" on page 98. Cut the border strips to fit and stitch them to the quilt top, mitering the corners.
5. Layer the quilt top with backing and batting; baste. Quilt as desired.
6. From binding fabric, cut 6 strips, each 2½" x 42". Sew them together with a diagonal seam (page 105) to make one piece of binding that is long enough for the quilt. Bind the edges of the quilt.

AIM FOR LOFTY HEIGHTS

by Deanna Spingola, 1994, Woodridge, Illinois, 49½" x 49½". Light in each of the four corners makes the center appear to float above the surface, creating a three-dimensional effect. This is the result of the advancing light values and the receding dark values.

FINISHED QUILT SIZE: 49½" x 49½" ✣ BLOCK SIZE: 10½"
BLOCKS: Eventual, Seville, Deseret ✣ SKILL LEVEL: Intermediate

Materials

DESIGN BLOCK	EVENTUAL	SEVILLE	DESERET
Strip Size	2" x 11"	2" x 11"	2" x 20"
	NO. OF STRIPS		
Dark Dark	17	13	12
Light Dark	8	11	0
Dark Medium	6	9	8
Light Medium	4	7	12
Dark Light	2	5	12
Light Light	12	4	5

44"-WIDE FABRIC

- ¾ yd. for border
- 3⅛ yds. for backing
- ½ yd. for binding
- 55" x 55" piece of batting

Strip Sets

Refer to "Making a Strip-Pieced Watercolor Quilt" on pages 19–25 for information on cutting and assembling strip sets and blocks.

Arrange the strips as shown below and sew them together. Make 1 of each strip set for each design block; label.

Eventual Blocks

Strip Set 1
Make 1.

Strip Set 2
Make 1.

Strip Set 3
Make 1.

Strip Set 4
Make 1.

Strip Set 5
Make 1.

Strip Set 6
Make 1.

Strip Set 7
Make 1.

Seville Blocks

Strip Set 1
Make 1.

Strip Set 2
Make 1.

Strip Set 3
Make 1.

Strip Set 4
Make 1.

Strip Set 5
Make 1.

Strip Set 6
Make 1.

Strip Set 7
Make 1.

Deseret Blocks

Strip Set 1
Make 1.

Strip Set 2
Make 1.

Strip Set 3
Make 1.

Strip Set 4
Make 1.

Strip Set 5
Make 1.

Strip Set 6
Make 1.

Strip Set 7
Make 1.

Block Construction

Stack the strip sets for the Eventual block in the proper order as described on pages 23–24 and cross-cut them into 4 segments, each 2" wide. Repeat with the strip sets for the Seville block. Stack and cut 8 segments, each 2" wide, for the Deseret blocks. Sew them together to make 4 Eventual blocks, 4 Seville blocks, and 8 Deseret blocks.

Press: U D U D U D U
Strip set #: 1 2 3 4 5 6 7

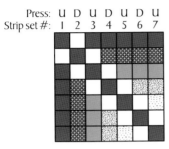

Block 1
Eventual
Make 4.

Press: U D U D U D U
Strip set #: 1 2 3 4 5 6 7

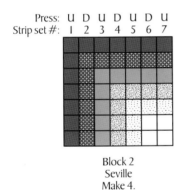

Block 2
Seville
Make 4.

Press: U D U D U D U
Strip set #: 1 2 3 4 5 6 7

Block 3
Deseret
Make 8.

Quilt Top Assembly

1. Arrange the blocks in 4 rows of 4 blocks each, referring to the quilt plan below. Alternate and rotate the blocks as necessary. Sew the blocks together as directed in "Assembling the Quilt Top" on page 97.

Dots on the quilt plan indicate the
upper left corner of the design block.

2. From border fabric, cut 6 strips, each 4" x 42".
3. Cut 2 border strips in half crosswise. Sew 1 strip to each of the remaining strips, using a diagonal seam as shown on pages 97–98.
4. Measure the quilt top for borders as described in "Making Borders with Mitered Corners" on page 98. Cut the border strips to fit and stitch them to the quilt top, mitering the corners.
5. Layer the quilt top with backing and batting; baste. Quilt as desired.
6. From binding fabric, cut 6 strips, each 2½" x 42". Sew them together with a diagonal seam (page 105) to make one piece of binding that is long enough for the quilt. Bind the edges of the quilt.

Stand in Holy Places

by Deanna Spingola, 1994, Woodridge, Illinois, 72" x 72". This high-contrast quilt combines in-the-ditch and stipple quilting and is reminiscent of a chapel window with the bright morning light filtering through.

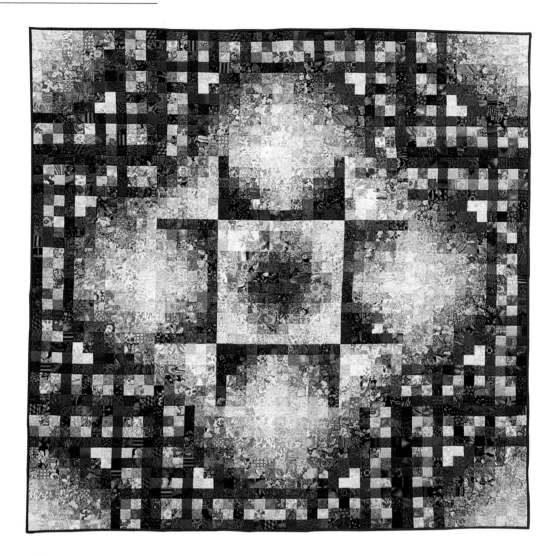

FINISHED QUILT SIZE: 72" x 72" ❖ BLOCK SIZE: 18"
BLOCKS: Twelve Square One, Boomerang ❖ SKILL LEVEL: Intermediate

Materials

Design Block	Twelve Square One	Boomerang
Strip Size	2" x 28"	2" x 11"
	NO. OF STRIPS	
Dark Dark	59	34
Light Dark	11	12
Dark Medium	29	26
Light Medium	13	26
Dark Light	23	34
Light Light	9	12

44"-WIDE FABRIC

- 4¼ yds. for backing
- ⅝ yd. for binding
- 78" x 78" piece of batting

Strip Sets

Refer to "Making a Strip-Pieced Watercolor Quilt" on pages 19–25 for information on cutting and assembling strip sets and blocks.

Arrange the strips as shown below and sew them together. Make 1 of each strip set for each design block; label.

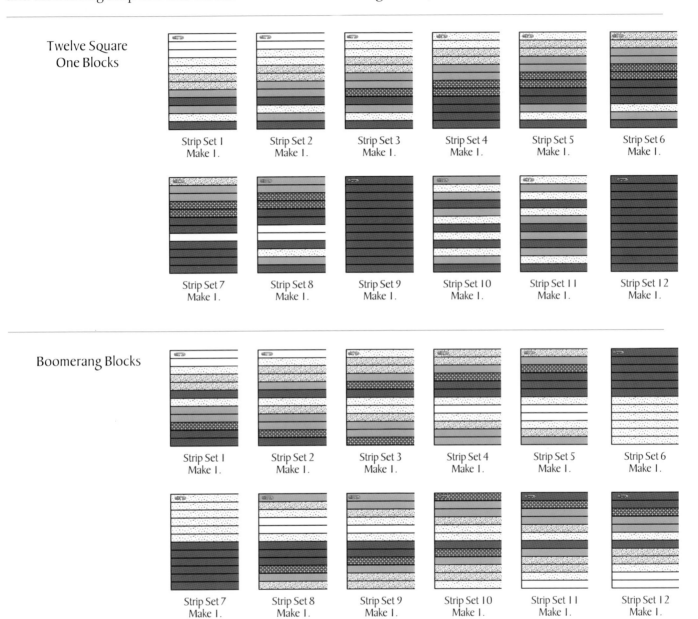

Twelve Square
One Blocks

Strip Set 1
Make 1.

Strip Set 2
Make 1.

Strip Set 3
Make 1.

Strip Set 4
Make 1.

Strip Set 5
Make 1.

Strip Set 6
Make 1.

Strip Set 7
Make 1.

Strip Set 8
Make 1.

Strip Set 9
Make 1.

Strip Set 10
Make 1.

Strip Set 11
Make 1.

Strip Set 12
Make 1.

Boomerang Blocks

Strip Set 1
Make 1.

Strip Set 2
Make 1.

Strip Set 3
Make 1.

Strip Set 4
Make 1.

Strip Set 5
Make 1.

Strip Set 6
Make 1.

Strip Set 7
Make 1.

Strip Set 8
Make 1.

Strip Set 9
Make 1.

Strip Set 10
Make 1.

Strip Set 11
Make 1.

Strip Set 12
Make 1.

Block Construction

Stack the strip sets for the Twelve Square One blocks in the proper order as described on pages 23–24 and crosscut them into 12 segments, each 2" wide. Stack and cut 4 segments, each 2" wide, for the Boomerang blocks. Sew the segments together to make 12 Twelve Square One blocks and 4 Boomerang blocks.

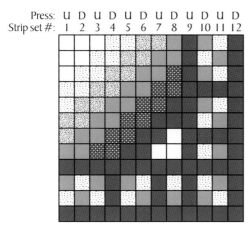

Press: U D U D U D U D U D U D
Strip set #: 1 2 3 4 5 6 7 8 9 10 11 12

Block 1
Twelve Square One
Make 12.

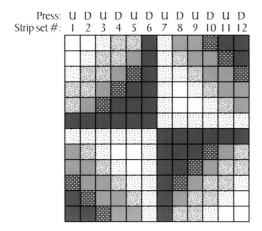

Press: U D U D U D U D U D U D
Strip set #: 1 2 3 4 5 6 7 8 9 10 11 12

Block 2
Boomerang
Make 4.

Quilt Top Assembly

1. Arrange the blocks in 4 rows of 4 blocks each, referring to the quilt plan below. Alternate and rotate the blocks as necessary. Sew the blocks together as directed in "Assembling the Quilt Top" on page 97.

Dots on the quilt plan indicate the upper left corner of the design block.

2. Layer the quilt top with backing and batting; baste. Quilt as desired.
3. From binding fabric, cut 7 strips, each 2½" x 42". Sew them together with a diagonal seam (page 105) to make one piece of binding that is long enough for the quilt. Bind the edges of the quilt.

GALAXY FIVE

by Mary Swanson and Laura Bushnell, 1994, Elmhurst, Illinois, 54" x 54". A relatively simple design block makes a dynamic quilt with the combination of bright colors and contrasting values. This machine-pieced and machine-quilted piece was a joint effort. So who gets custody?

FINISHED QUILT SIZE: 54" x 54" ◈ BLOCK SIZE: 7½"
BLOCK: Armitage ◈ SKILL LEVEL: Beginner

Materials

2" x 42" STRIPS		
■ Dark Dark	10
▨ Light Dark	10
▨ Dark Medium	12
▨ Light Medium	6
▫ Dark Light	4
□ Light Light	8

44"-WIDE FABRIC

- ⅓ yd. for inner border
- ⅝ yd. for outer border
- 3⅓ yds. for backing
- ½ yd. for binding
- 60" x 60" piece of batting

Strip Sets

Refer to "Making a Strip-Pieced Watercolor Quilt" on pages 19–25 for information on cutting and assembling strip sets and blocks.

Make 2 identical strip sets for each of the strip sets required, or make them from different groups of fabrics. If you choose to make identical strip sets, you will need only half the number of fabrics listed, but you will need 2 strips of each fabric.

Arrange the strips as shown below and sew them together. Make 2 of each strip set; label.

Armitage Blocks

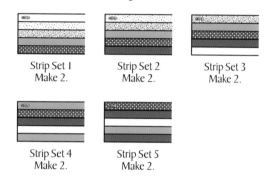

Strip Set 1
Make 2.

Strip Set 2
Make 2.

Strip Set 3
Make 2.

Strip Set 4
Make 2.

Strip Set 5
Make 2.

Block Construction

Stack 1 group of strip sets in the proper order as described on pages 23–24 and crosscut 18 segments, each 2" wide. Stack and cut 18 segments from the remaining group of strip sets. Sew the segments together as shown to make 36 blocks.

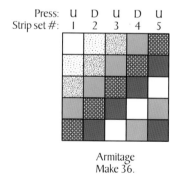

Press: U   D   U   D   U
Strip set #: 1   2   3   4   5

Armitage
Make 36.

Quilt Top Assembly

1. Arrange the blocks in 6 rows of 6 blocks each, referring to the quilt plan below and rotating the blocks as necessary. Sew the blocks together as directed in "Assembling the Quilt Top" on page 97.

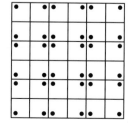

Dots on the quilt plan indicate the upper left corner of the design block.

2. From the inner border fabric, cut 6 strips, each 1½" x 42". Cut 6 strips, each 2¾" x 42", from outer border fabric.

3. Sew each inner border strip to an outer border strip. Press the seam toward the outer border strip. Cut 2 of these border strips in half crosswise. Sew 1 piece to each remaining strip, using a diagonal seam as shown on pages 97–98.

4. Measure the quilt top for borders as described in "Making Borders with Mitered Corners" on page 98. Cut the border strips to fit and stitch them to the quilt top, mitering the corners.

5. Layer the quilt top with backing and batting; baste. Quilt as desired. Trim backing and batting 1½" away from the raw edge of the border.

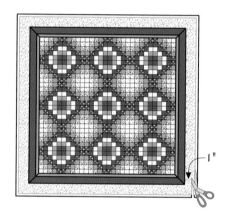

1"

6. From binding fabric, cut 6 strips, each 2½" x 42". Sew them together with a diagonal seam (page 105) to make one piece of binding that is long enough for the quilt. Fold over and press ⅜" on one long side of the binding strip. Pin the raw, unfolded edge of the binding to the raw edge of the border. Stitch in place, mitering the corners. This binding will finish to 1" wide.

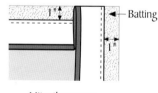

1"   Batting

1"

Miter the corner.

7. Fold the binding to the back over the edge of the extended batting and backing and hand stitch it to the wrong side of the quilt, mitering the corners.

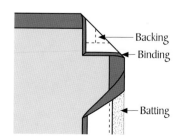

Backing

Binding

Batting

$\mathcal{M}$IA MARIE'S MAZE

by Deanna Spingola, 1994, Woodridge, Illinois, 48" x 48". Random columns of confetti and pockets of flowers make it harder to find your way through this maze. A butterfly-print border aptly frames this lap quilt.

FINISHED QUILT SIZE: 48" x 48" ❖ BLOCK SIZE: 13½"
BLOCK: Nine Square Two ❖ SKILL LEVEL: Beginner

Materials

2" x 22" STRIPS	
▉ Dark Dark	9
▣ Light Dark	18
▦ Dark Medium	15
▢ Light Medium	12
▢ Dark Light	18
☐ Light Light	9

44"-WIDE FABRIC

- ■ ⅓ yd. for inner border
- ■ ⅝ yd. for outer border
- ■ 3 yds. for backing
- ■ ½ yd. for binding
- ■ 54" x 54" piece of batting

Strip Sets

Refer to "Making a Strip-Pieced Watercolor Quilt" on pages 19–25 for information on cutting and assembling strip sets and blocks.

Arrange the strips as shown below and sew them together. Make 1 of each strip set; label.

Nine Square Two Blocks

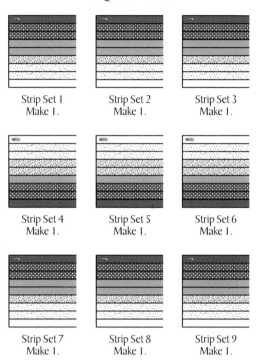

Strip Set 1
Make 1.

Strip Set 2
Make 1.

Strip Set 3
Make 1.

Strip Set 4
Make 1.

Strip Set 5
Make 1.

Strip Set 6
Make 1.

Strip Set 7
Make 1.

Strip Set 8
Make 1.

Strip Set 9
Make 1.

Block Construction

Stack the strip sets in the proper order as described on pages 23–24 and crosscut them into 9 segments, each 2" wide. Sew the segments together to make 9 blocks.

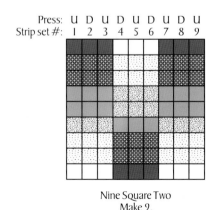

Press: U D U D U D U D U
Strip set #: 1 2 3 4 5 6 7 8 9

Nine Square Two
Make 9.

Quilt Top Assembly

1. Arrange the blocks in 3 rows of 3 blocks each, referring to the quilt plan below and rotating the blocks as necessary. Sew the blocks together as directed in "Assembling the Quilt Top" on page 97.

Dots on the quilt plan indicate the upper left corner of the design block.

2. From the inner border fabric, cut 6 strips, each 1½" x 42". Cut 6 strips, each 3" x 42", from outer border fabric.

3. Sew each inner border strip to an outer border strip. Press the seam toward the outer border strip. Cut 2 of the resulting border strips in half crosswise. Sew 1 short strip to each of the remaining strips, using a diagonal seam as shown on pages 97–98.

4. Measure the quilt top for borders as described in "Making Borders with Mitered Corners" on page 98. Cut the border strips to fit and stitch them to the quilt top, mitering the corners.

5. Layer the quilt top with backing and batting; baste. Quilt as desired.

6. From binding fabric, cut 6 strips, each 2½" x 42". Sew them together with a diagonal seam (page 105) to make one piece of binding that is long enough for the quilt. Bind the edges of the quilt.

ℛoses All in a Row

by Linda Garzinski, 1995, Downers Grove, Illinois, 63" x 63". The light values advance and provide a sharp contrast in this predominantly dark-value quilt. It is machine quilted with an allover meandering design.

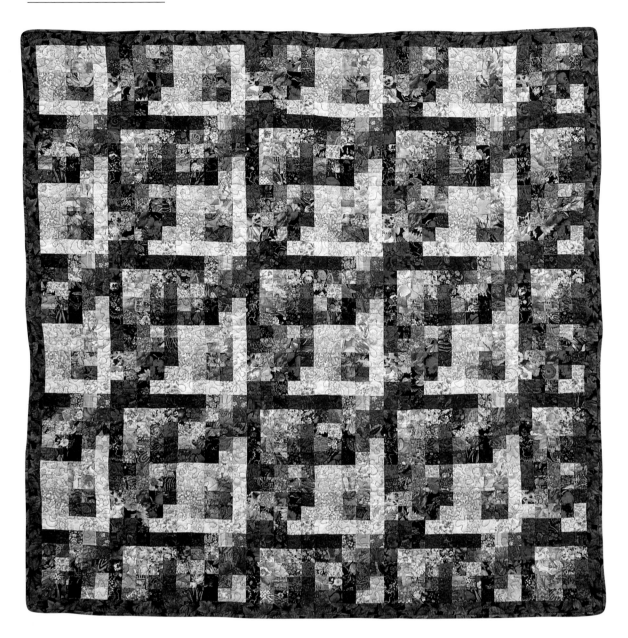

FINISHED QUILT SIZE: 63" x 63" ❖ BLOCK SIZE: 15" ❖ BLOCK: Sioux ❖ SKILL LEVEL: Intermediate

Materials

2" x 42" STRIPS		
■ Dark Dark		33
▦ Light Dark		15
▨ Dark Medium		13
▨ Light Medium		15
▢ Dark Light		12
☐ Light Light		12

44"-WIDE FABRIC

- ½ yd. for border
- 4 yds. for backing
- ⅝ yd. for binding
- 72" x 72" piece of batting

Strip Sets

Refer to "Making a Strip-Pieced Watercolor Quilt" on pages 19–25 for information on cutting and assembling strip sets and blocks.

Arrange the strips as shown below and sew them together. Make 1 of each strip set; label.

Sioux Blocks

Strip Set 1
Make 1.

Strip Set 2
Make 1.

Strip Set 3
Make 1.

Strip Set 4
Make 1.

Strip Set 5
Make 1.

Strip Set 6
Make 1.

Strip Set 7
Make 1.

Strip Set 8
Make 1.

Strip Set 9
Make 1.

Strip Set 10
Make 1.

Block Construction

Stack the strip sets in the proper order as described on pages 23–24 and crosscut them into 16 segments, each 2" wide. Sew the segments together to make 16 blocks.

Note: The strip sets are long enough to make 4 additional blocks. Construct these extra blocks and reserve them to make "A Miniature Flower Garden" on page 65.

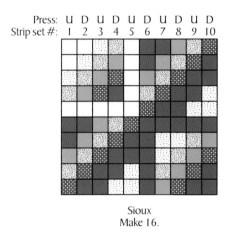

Press:	U	D	U	D	U	D	U	D	U	D
Strip set #:	1	2	3	4	5	6	7	8	9	10

Sioux
Make 16.

Quilt Top Assembly

1. Arrange the blocks in 4 rows of 4 blocks each, referring to the quilt plan below.

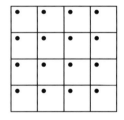

Dots on the quilt plan indicate the upper left corner of the design block.

2. From border fabric, cut 8 strips, each 2" x 42".
3. Sew pairs of border strips together, end to end, with a diagonal seam as shown on pages 97–98 to make 4 identical borders.
4. Measure the quilt top for borders as described in "Making Borders with Mitered Corners" on page 98. Cut the border strips to fit and stitch them to the quilt top, mitering the corners.
5. Layer the quilt top with backing and batting; baste. Quilt as desired.
6. From binding fabric, cut 8 strips, each 2½" x 42". Sew them together with a diagonal seam (page 105) to make one piece of binding that is long enough for the quilt. Bind the edges of the quilt.

A MINIATURE FLOWER GARDEN

by Linda Garzinski, 1995, Downers Grove, Illinois, 30½" x 30½". Waste not, want not. This wall hanging was created with four of the Sioux blocks left over from the "Roses All in a Row" quilt. Dark values predominate with just enough of the light values to add interest.

FINISHED QUILT SIZE: 30½" x 30½" ❖ BLOCK SIZE: 15" ❖ BLOCK: Sioux ❖ SKILL LEVEL: Intermediate

Materials

2" x 11" STRIPS		44"-WIDE FABRIC
Dark Dark	33	■ 1 yd. for backing
Light Dark	15	■ ⅓ yd. for binding
Dark Medium	13	■ 36" x 36" piece of batting
Light Medium	15	
Dark Light	12	
Light Light	12	

Strip Sets

Refer to "Making a Strip-Pieced Watercolor Quilt" on pages 19–25 for information on cutting and assembling strip sets and blocks.

Use the 4 blocks remaining from "Roses All in a Row" on page 00 to create this wall hanging, or construct new strip sets. Arrange the strips as shown below and sew them together. Make 1 of each strip set; label.

Sioux Blocks

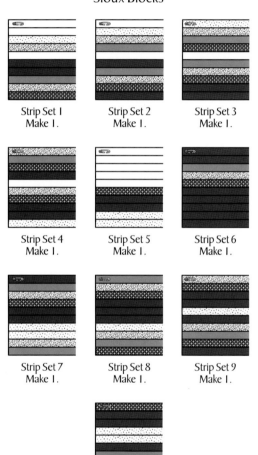

Strip Set 1
Make 1.

Strip Set 2
Make 1.

Strip Set 3
Make 1.

Strip Set 4
Make 1.

Strip Set 5
Make 1.

Strip Set 6
Make 1.

Strip Set 7
Make 1.

Strip Set 8
Make 1.

Strip Set 9
Make 1.

Strip Set 10
Make 1.

Block Construction

Stack the strip sets in the proper order as described on pages 23–24 and crosscut them into 4 segments, each 2" wide. Sew the segments together to make 4 blocks.

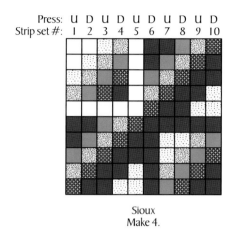

Press: U D U D U D U D U D
Strip set #: 1 2 3 4 5 6 7 8 9 10

Sioux
Make 4.

Quilt Top Assembly

1. Arrange the blocks in 2 rows of 2 blocks each, referring to the quilt plan below and rotating the blocks as necessary. Sew the blocks together as directed in "Assembling the Quilt Top" on page 97.

Dots on the quilt plan indicate the upper left corner of the design block.

2. Layer the quilt top with backing and batting; baste. Quilt as desired.
3. From binding fabric, cut 4 strips, each 2½" x 42". Sew them together with a diagonal seam (page 105) to make one piece of binding that is long enough for the quilt. Bind the edges of the quilt.

THE HEARTS
OF THE CHILDREN

by Carol Sherwood, 1995, Bolingbrook, Illinois, 34" x 34".
Four hearts represent Carol's four wonderful children. The
hearts feature warm colors on the interior and dark value
prints on the exterior. A warm red inner border frames this
hand-quilted wall hanging.

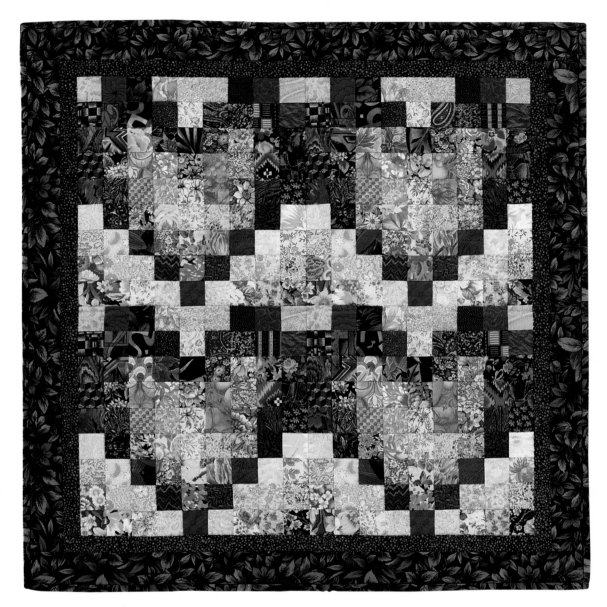

FINISHED QUILT SIZE: 34" x 34" ✦ BLOCK SIZE: 13½" ✦ BLOCK: Heart ✦ SKILL LEVEL: Beginner

Materials

2" x 11" STRIPS		
■ Dark Dark	22
▦ Light Dark	10
■ Dark Medium	12
▨ Light Medium	15
▫ Dark Light	14
□ Light Light	8

44"-WIDE FABRIC

- ¼ yd. for inner border
- ⅓ yd. for outer border
- 1⅛ yds. for backing
- ⅓ yd. for binding
- 41" x 41" piece of batting

Strip Sets

Refer to "Making a Strip-Pieced Watercolor Quilt" on pages 19–25 for information on cutting and assembling strip sets and blocks.

Arrange the strips as shown below and sew them together. Make 1 of each strip set; label.

Heart Blocks

Strip Set 1
Make 1.

Strip Set 2
Make 1.

Strip Set 3
Make 1.

Strip Set 4
Make 1.

Strip Set 5
Make 1.

Strip Set 6
Make 1.

Strip Set 7
Make 1.

Strip Set 8
Make 1.

Strip Set 9
Make 1.

Quilt Top Assembly

1. Arrange the blocks in 2 rows of 2 blocks each, referring to the quilt plan below. Sew the blocks together as directed in "Assembling the Quilt Top" on page 97.

Dots on the quilt plan indicate the upper left corner of the design block.

2. From the inner border fabric, cut 4 strips, each 1½" x 42". Cut 4 strips, each 2¾" x 42", from outer border fabric.
3. Sew each inner border strip to an outer border strip. Press the seams toward the outer border strip.
4. Measure the quilt top for borders as described in "Making Borders with Mitered Corners" on page 98. Cut the border strips to fit and stitch them to the quilt top, mitering the corners.
5. Layer the quilt top with backing and batting; baste. Quilt as desired.
6. From binding fabric, cut 4 strips, each 2½" x 42". Sew them together with a diagonal seam (page 105) to make one piece of binding that is long enough for the quilt. Bind the edges of the quilt.

Block Construction

Stack the strip sets in the proper order as described on pages 23–24 and crosscut them into 4 segments, each 2" wide. Sew the segments together to make 4 blocks.

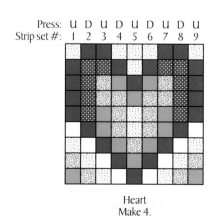

Press: U D U D U D U D U
Strip set #: 1 2 3 4 5 6 7 8 9

Heart
Make 4.

by Trisha Horner, 1995, Normal, Illinois, 49" x 49". This simple block makes a stunning lap or wall quilt. It is machine quilted.

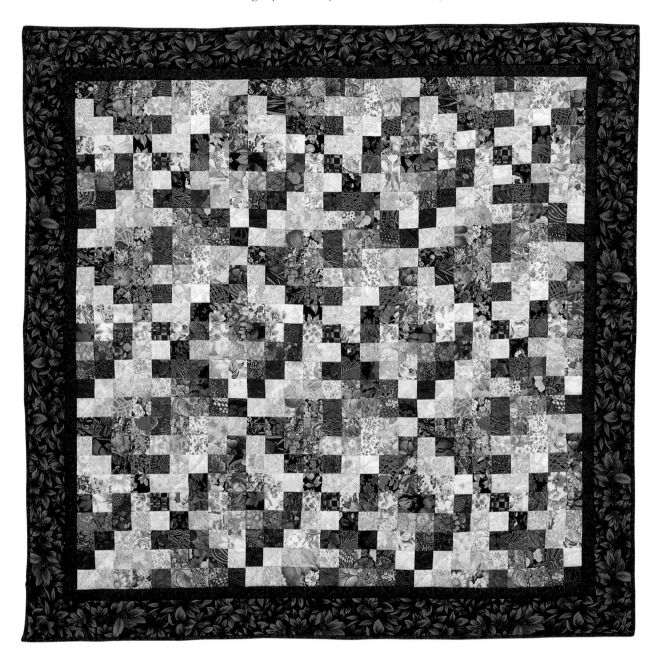

FINISHED QUILT SIZE: 49" x 49" ❖ BLOCK SIZE: 13½" ❖ BLOCK: Zigzag ❖ SKILL LEVEL: Beginner

Materials

2" x 22" STRIPS		
■ Dark Dark	23	
▦ Light Dark	10	
■ Dark Medium	8	
▒ Light Medium	8	
⬚ Dark Light	10	
□ Light Light	22	

44"-WIDE FABRIC

- ¼ yd. for inner border
- ½ yd. for outer border
- 3 yds. for backing
- ½ yd. for binding
- 54" x 54" piece of batting

Strip Sets

Refer to "Making a Strip-Pieced Watercolor Quilt" on pages 19–25 for information on cutting and assembling strip sets and blocks.

Arrange the strips as shown below and sew them together. Make 1 of each strip set; label.

Zigzag Blocks

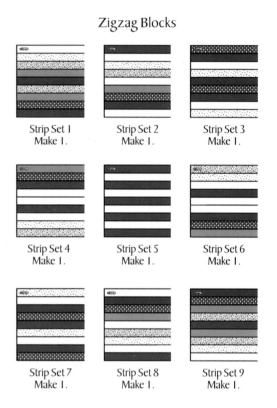

Strip Set 1
Make 1.

Strip Set 2
Make 1.

Strip Set 3
Make 1.

Strip Set 4
Make 1.

Strip Set 5
Make 1.

Strip Set 6
Make 1.

Strip Set 7
Make 1.

Strip Set 8
Make 1.

Strip Set 9
Make 1.

Block Construction

Stack the strip sets in the proper order as described on pages 23–24 and crosscut them into 9 segments, each 2" wide. Sew the segments together to make 9 blocks.

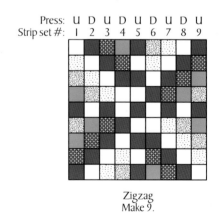

Press: U D U D U D U D U
Strip set #: 1 2 3 4 5 6 7 8 9

Zigzag
Make 9.

Quilt Top Assembly

1. Arrange the blocks in 3 rows of 3 blocks each, referring to the quilt plan below. Sew the blocks together as directed in "Assembling the Quilt Top" on page 97.

Dots on the quilt plan indicate the upper left corner of the design block.

2. From the inner border fabric, cut 6 strips, each 1½" x 42". Cut 6 strips, each 3½" x 42", from outer border fabric. Sew each inner border strip to an outer border strip. Press the seams toward the outer border strip. Cut 2 of the resulting strips in half crosswise. Sew 1 strip to each of the remaining strips, using a diagonal seam as shown on pages 97–98.

3. Measure the quilt top for borders as described in "Making Borders with Mitered Corners" on page 98. Cut the border strips to fit and stitch them to the quilt top, mitering the corners.

4. Layer the quilt top with backing and batting; baste. Quilt as desired.

5. From binding fabric, cut 6 strips, each 2½" x 42". Sew them together with a diagonal seam (page 105) to make one piece of binding that is long enough for the quilt. Bind the edges of the quilt.

LAUREN'S WINDMILL

by Deanna Spingola, 1994, Woodridge, Illinois, 36" x 36". Warm colors predominate in this sunny version of a favorite pattern. Floral confetti is apparent in the paddles of the windmill.

FINISHED QUILT SIZE: 36" x 36" ❖ BLOCK SIZE: 13½" ❖ BLOCK: Nine Square One ❖ SKILL LEVEL: Beginner

Materials

2" X 11" STRIPS		
■ Dark Dark	10
▨ Light Dark	11
■ Dark Medium	15
▨ Light Medium	24
▨ Dark Light	11
☐ Light Light	10

44"-WIDE FABRIC

- ¼ yd. for inner border
- ½ yd. for outer border
- 1⅛ yds. for backing
- ⅓ yd. for binding
- 40" x 40" piece of batting

Strip Sets

Refer to "Making a Strip-Pieced Watercolor Quilt" on pages 19–25 for information on cutting and assembling strip sets and blocks.

Arrange the strips as shown below and sew them together. Make 1 of each strip set; label.

Nine Square One Blocks

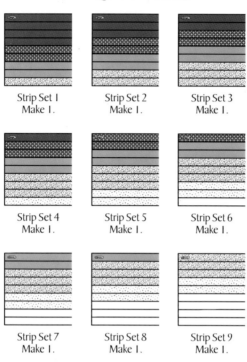

Strip Set 1
Make 1.

Strip Set 2
Make 1.

Strip Set 3
Make 1.

Strip Set 4
Make 1.

Strip Set 5
Make 1.

Strip Set 6
Make 1.

Strip Set 7
Make 1.

Strip Set 8
Make 1.

Strip Set 9
Make 1.

Block Construction

Stack the strip sets in the proper order as described on pages 23–24 and crosscut them into 4 segments, each 2" wide. Sew the segments together to make 4 blocks.

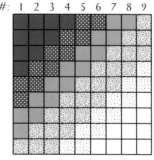

Press: U D U D U D U D U
Strip set #: 1 2 3 4 5 6 7 8 9

Nine Square One
Make 4.

Quilt Top Assembly

1. Arrange the blocks in 2 rows of 2 blocks each, referring to the quilt plan below and rotating the blocks as necessary. Sew the blocks together as directed in "Assembling the Quilt Top" on page 97.

Dots on the quilt plan indicate the upper left corner of the design block.

2. From the inner border fabric, cut 4 strips, each 1½" x 42". Cut 4 strips, each 3¾" x 42", from outer border fabric.
3. Sew each inner border strip to an outer border strip. Press seams toward the outer border strip.
4. Measure the quilt top for borders as described in "Making Borders with Mitered Corners" on page 98. Cut the border strips to fit and stitch them to the quilt top, mitering the corners.
5. Layer the quilt top with backing and batting; baste. Quilt as desired.
6. From binding fabric, cut 4 strips, each 2½" x 42". Sew them together with a diagonal seam (page 105) to make one piece of binding that is long enough for the quilt. Bind the edges of the quilt.

WHO KNOWS?

by Carol Deal, 1994, Bloomington, Illinois, 62½" x 62½". This quilt is full of light and motion, just like a garden in the spring. "Tic Tac Toe" (page 26) was made from the same blocks, but the arrangement is different. Which do you like best?

FINISHED QUILT SIZE: 62½" x 62½"   ❖   BLOCK SIZE: 13½"
BLOCKS: Dark Line, Light Line   ❖   SKILL LEVEL: Intermediate

Materials

DESIGN BLOCK	DARK LINE	LIGHT LINE
Strip Size	2" x 20"	2" x 20"
	NO. OF STRIPS	
Dark Dark	9	6
Light Dark	16	14
Dark Medium	14	10
Light Medium	22	26
Dark Light	14	16
Light Light	6	9

44"-WIDE FABRIC

- ¾ yd. for border
- 3¾ yds. for backing
- ½ yd. for binding
- 68" x 68" piece of batting

Strip Sets

Refer to "Making a Strip-Pieced Watercolor Quilt" on pages 19–25 for information on cutting and assembling strip sets and blocks.

Arrange the strips as shown below and sew them together. Make 1 of each strip set for each design block; label.

Dark Line Blocks

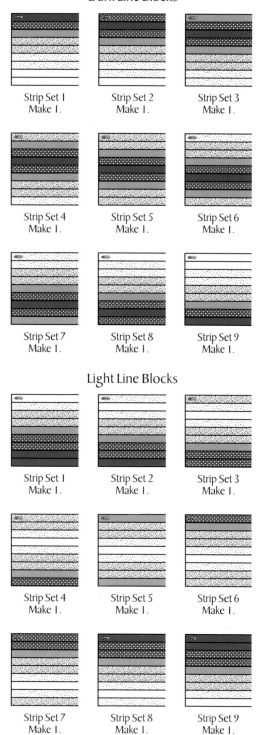

Strip Set 1
Make 1.

Strip Set 2
Make 1.

Strip Set 3
Make 1.

Strip Set 4
Make 1.

Strip Set 5
Make 1.

Strip Set 6
Make 1.

Strip Set 7
Make 1.

Strip Set 8
Make 1.

Strip Set 9
Make 1.

Light Line Blocks

Strip Set 1
Make 1.

Strip Set 2
Make 1.

Strip Set 3
Make 1.

Strip Set 4
Make 1.

Strip Set 5
Make 1.

Strip Set 6
Make 1.

Strip Set 7
Make 1.

Strip Set 8
Make 1.

Strip Set 9
Make 1.

Block Construction

Stack the strip sets for the Dark Line block in the proper order as described on pages 23–24 and crosscut them into 8 segments, each 2" wide. Repeat with the strip sets for the Light Line block. Sew the segments together to make 8 Dark Line blocks and 8 Light Line blocks.

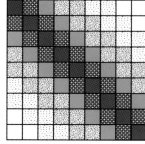

Block 1
Dark Line
Make 8.

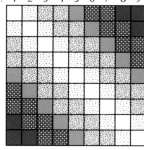

Block 2
Light Line
Make 8.

Quilt Top Assembly

1. Arrange the blocks in 4 rows of 4 blocks each, referring to the quilt plan at right. Sew the blocks together as directed in "Assembling the Quilt Top" on page 97.

2	1	2	1
1	2	1	2
2	1	2	1
1	2	1	2

   Dots on the quilt plan indicate the upper left corner of the design block.

2. From border fabric, cut 6 strips, each 4½" x 42". Cut 2 strips in half crosswise. Sew 1 strip to each of the remaining strips, using a diagonal seam as shown on pages 97–98.

3. Measure the quilt top for borders as described in "Borders with Straight-Cut Corners" on page 99. Cut 2 strips to fit and stitch them to opposite side edges of the quilt top. Press seams toward the borders. Trim the 2 remaining strips to fit the top and bottom edges and sew them to the quilt top.

4. Layer the quilt top with backing and batting; baste. Quilt as desired.

5. From binding fabric, cut 6 strips, each 2½" x 42". Sew them together with a diagonal seam (page 105) to make one piece of binding that is long enough for the quilt. Bind the edges of the quilt.

# XCITING

by Doris Havens, 1994, Bolingbrook, Illinois 32½" x 32½". What is more exciting than creating a work of art for the wall? Blue marks the spot on this little wall hanging.

FINISHED QUILT SIZE: 32½" x 32½" ◈ BLOCK SIZE: 13½" ◈ BLOCK: Dark Line ◈ SKILL LEVEL: Beginner

Materials

2" X 11" STRIPS		
▓	Dark Dark	9
▦	Light Dark	16
▨	Dark Medium	14
▦	Light Medium	22
░	Dark Light	14
☐	Light Light	6

44"-WIDE FABRIC

- ½ yd. for border
- 1⅛ yds. for backing
- ⅓ yd. for binding
- 38" x 38" piece of batting

Strip Sets

Refer to "Making a Strip-Pieced Watercolor Quilt" on pages 19–25 for information on cutting and assembling strip sets and blocks.

Arrange the strips as shown below and sew them together. Make 1 of each strip set; label.

Dark Line Blocks

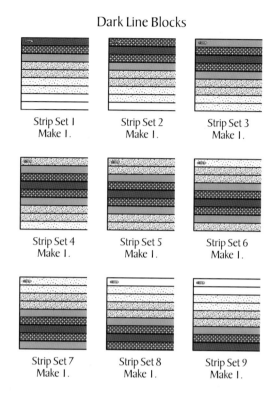

Strip Set 1
Make 1.

Strip Set 2
Make 1.

Strip Set 3
Make 1.

Strip Set 4
Make 1.

Strip Set 5
Make 1.

Strip Set 6
Make 1.

Strip Set 7
Make 1.

Strip Set 8
Make 1.

Strip Set 9
Make 1.

Block Construction

Stack the strip sets in the proper order as described on pages 23–24 and crosscut them into 4 segments, each 2" wide. Sew the segments together to make 4 blocks.

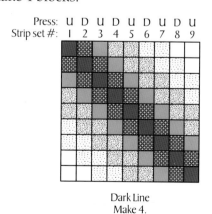

Press: U D U D U D U D U
Strip set #: 1 2 3 4 5 6 7 8 9

Dark Line
Make 4.

Quilt Top Assembly

1. Arrange the blocks in 2 rows of 2 blocks each, referring to the quilt plan below and rotating the blocks as necessary. Sew the blocks together as directed in "Assembling the Quilt Top" on page 97.

Dots on the quilt plan indicate the upper left corner of the design block.

2. From border fabric, cut 4 strips, each 3" x 42".
3. Measure the quilt top for borders as described in "Making Borders with Mitered Corners" on page 98. Cut the border strips to fit and stitch them to the quilt top, mitering the corners.
5. Layer the quilt top with backing and batting; baste. Quilt as desired.
6. From binding fabric, cut 4 strips, each 2½" x 42". Sew them together with a diagonal seam (page 105) to make one piece of binding that is long enough for the quilt. Bind the edges of the quilt.

$\mathcal{L}$ET'S PLAY BALL!

by Paulette Hinton, 1994, Edwardsville, Illinois, 35½" x 35½". Reminiscent of a baseball diamond, this design was created during the 1994 baseball strike.

FINISHED QUILT SIZE: 35½" x 35½" ✤ BLOCK SIZE: 15" ✤ BLOCK: Nevada ✤ SKILL LEVEL: Beginner

Materials

2" x 11" STRIPS			44"-WIDE FABRIC
■ Dark Dark	20		■ ½ yd. for border
▦ Light Dark	22		■ 1⅛ yds. for backing
▨ Dark Medium	19		■ ⅓ yd. for binding
▧ Light Medium	16		■ 41" x 41" piece of batting
▨ Dark Light	13		
□ Light Light	10		

Strip Sets

Refer to "Making a Strip-Pieced Watercolor Quilt" on pages 19–25 for information on cutting and assembling strip sets and blocks.

Arrange the strips as shown below and sew them together. Make 1 of each strip set; label.

Nevada Blocks

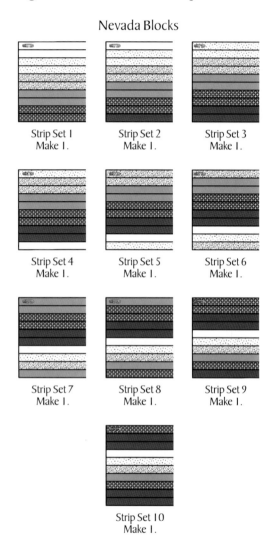

Strip Set 1
Make 1.

Strip Set 2
Make 1.

Strip Set 3
Make 1.

Strip Set 4
Make 1.

Strip Set 5
Make 1.

Strip Set 6
Make 1.

Strip Set 7
Make 1.

Strip Set 8
Make 1.

Strip Set 9
Make 1.

Strip Set 10
Make 1.

Block Construction

Stack the strip sets in the proper order as described on pages 23–24 and crosscut them into 4 segments, each 2" wide. Sew the segments together to make 4 blocks.

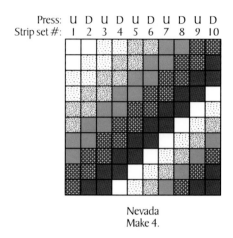

Nevada
Make 4.

Quilt Top Assembly

1. Arrange the blocks in 2 rows of 2 blocks each, referring to the quilt plan below and rotating the blocks as necessary. Sew the blocks together as directed in "Assembling the Quilt Top" on page 97.

Dots on the quilt plan indicate the upper left corner of the design block.

2. From border fabric, cut 4 strips, each 3" x 42".
3. Measure the quilt top for borders as described in "Making Borders with Straight-Cut Corners" on page 99. Cut 2 border strips to fit and stitch them to opposite side edges of the quilt top. Press seams toward the borders. Measure the quilt for top and bottom borders, trim 2 strips to fit, and sew them to the top and bottom edges of the quilt top.
4. Layer the quilt top with backing and batting; baste. Quilt as desired.
5. From binding fabric, cut 4 strips, each 2½" x 42". Sew them together with a diagonal seam (page 105) to make one piece of binding that is long enough for the quilt. Bind the edges of the quilt.

MEDIATOR IN THE CABIN

by Marilyn Luccese, 1995, Ankeny, Iowa, 44" x 44". This colorful quilt, reminiscent of a Log Cabin design, is machine quilted with the radiating lines extending into the border.

FINISHED QUILT SIZE: 44" x 44" ❖ BLOCK SIZE: 12" ❖ BLOCK: Mediator ❖ SKILL LEVEL: Beginner

Materials

2" X 22" STRIPS			44"-WIDE FABRIC
■	Dark Dark	8	■ ¼ yd. for inner border
▨	Light Dark	10	■ ⅝ yd. for outer border
▦	Dark Medium	14	■ 2⅔ yds. for backing
▨	Light Medium	14	■ ½ yd. for binding
▨	Dark Light	10	■ 47" x 47" piece of batting
□	Light Light	8	

Strip Sets

Refer to "Making a Strip-Pieced Watercolor Quilt" on pages 19–25 for information on cutting and assembling strip sets and blocks.

Arrange the strips as shown below and sew them together. Make 1 of each strip set; label.

Mediator Blocks

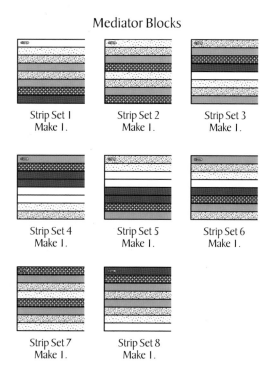

Strip Set 1
Make 1.

Strip Set 2
Make 1.

Strip Set 3
Make 1.

Strip Set 4
Make 1.

Strip Set 5
Make 1.

Strip Set 6
Make 1.

Strip Set 7
Make 1.

Strip Set 8
Make 1.

Block Construction

Stack the strip sets in the proper order as described on pages 23–24 and crosscut them into 9 segments, each 2" wide. Sew the segments together to make 9 blocks.

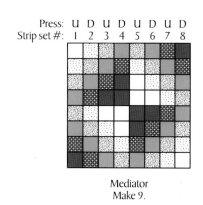

Press: U D U D U D U D
Strip set #: 1 2 3 4 5 6 7 8

Mediator
Make 9.

Quilt Top Assembly

1. Arrange the blocks in 3 rows of 3 blocks each, referring to the quilt plan below. Sew the blocks together as directed in "Assembling the Quilt Top" on page 97.

Dots on the quilt plan indicate the upper left corner of the design block.

2. From the inner border fabric, cut 6 strips, each 1½ x 42". Cut 6 strips, each 3¼" x 42", from outer border fabric. Sew each inner border strip to an outer border strip. Press the seam toward the inner border strip.

3. Cut 2 of the resulting border strips in half crosswise. Sew 1 short strip to each of the remaining strips, using a diagonal seam as shown on pages 97–98. Make 4 border strips.

4. Measure the quilt top for borders as described in "Making Borders with Mitered Corners" on page 98. Cut the border strips to fit and stitch them to the quilt top, mitering the corners.

5. Layer the quilt top with backing and batting; baste. Quilt as desired.

6. From binding fabric, cut 6 strips, each 2½" x 42". Sew them together with a diagonal seam (page 105) to make 1 piece of binding that is long enough for the quilt. Bind the edges of the quilt.

CATALPA

by Pamella Gray, 1995, Dousman, Wisconsin, 44½" x 44½". Warm and cool colors mingle in this lap quilt, while three-dimensional cubes skip above the surface. The inner border picks up colors that march through the interior of the quilt.

FINISHED QUILT SIZE: 44½" x 44½" ❖ BLOCK SIZE: 12"
BLOCKS: Mediator, Goodness ❖ SKILL LEVEL: Intermediate

Materials

DESIGN BLOCK	MEDIATOR	GOODNESS
Strip Size	2" x 13"	2" x 11"
	NO. OF STRIPS	
Dark Dark	8	11
Light Dark	10	12
Dark Medium	14	11
Light Medium	14	11
Dark Light	10	10
Light Light	8	9

44"-WIDE FABRIC

- ⅓ yd. for inner border
- ¾ yd. for outer border
- 2¾ yds. for backing
- ½ yd. for binding
- 50" x 50" piece of batting

Strip Sets

Refer to "Making a Strip-Pieced Watercolor Quilt" on pages 19–25 for information on cutting and assembling strip sets and blocks.

Arrange the strips as shown below and sew them together. Make 1 of each strip set for each design block; label.

Mediator Blocks

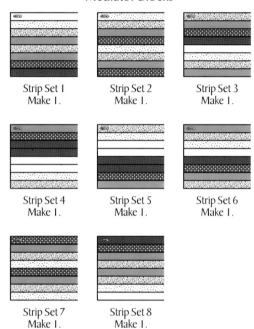

Strip Set 1
Make 1.

Strip Set 2
Make 1.

Strip Set 3
Make 1.

Strip Set 4
Make 1.

Strip Set 5
Make 1.

Strip Set 6
Make 1.

Strip Set 7
Make 1.

Strip Set 8
Make 1.

Goodness Blocks

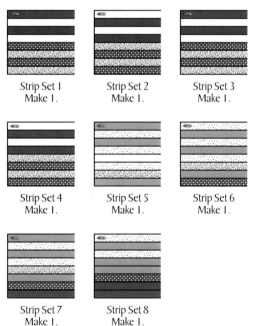

Strip Set 1
Make 1.

Strip Set 2
Make 1.

Strip Set 3
Make 1.

Strip Set 4
Make 1.

Strip Set 5
Make 1.

Strip Set 6
Make 1.

Strip Set 7
Make 1.

Strip Set 8
Make 1.

Block Construction

Stack the strip sets for the Mediator block in the proper order as described on pages 23–24 and crosscut them into 5 segments, each 2" wide. Stack and cut 4 segments, each 2" wide, for the Goodness block. Sew the segments together to make 5 Mediator and 4 Goodness blocks.

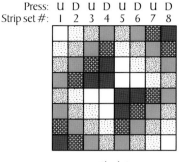

Press: U D U D U D U D
Strip set #: 1 2 3 4 5 6 7 8

Block 1
Mediator
Make 5.

Press: U D U D U D U D
Strip set #: 1 2 3 4 5 6 7 8

Block 2
Goodness
Make 4.

Quilt Top Assembly

1. Arrange the blocks in 3 rows of 3 blocks each, referring to the quilt plan at right. Sew them together as directed in "Assembling the Quilt Top" on page 97.

   Dots on the quilt plan indicate the upper left corner of the design block.

2. From the inner border fabric, cut 6 strips, each 1½" x 42". Cut 6 strips, each 3½" x 42", from outer border fabric.

3. Sew each inner border strip to an outer border strip. Press the seam toward the outer border strip. Cut 2 of the resulting border strips in half crosswise. Sew 1 short strip to each of the remaining strips, using a diagonal seam as shown on pages 97–98.

4. Measure the quilt top for borders as described in "Making Borders with Mitered Corners" on page 98. Cut the border strips to fit and stitch them to the quilt top, mitering the corners.

5. Layer the quilt top with backing and batting; baste. Quilt as desired.

6. From binding fabric, cut 5 strips, each 2½" x 42". Sew them together with a diagonal seam (page 105) to make one piece of binding that is long enough for the quilt. Bind the edges of the quilt.

$\mathcal{C}$ALVARY

by Martha Mueller, 1995, Chicago, Illinois, 40" x 40". The dark value provides high contrast with the light value. A wreath of spring flowers surrounds the cross. The quilt is skillfully hand quilted with metallic thread.

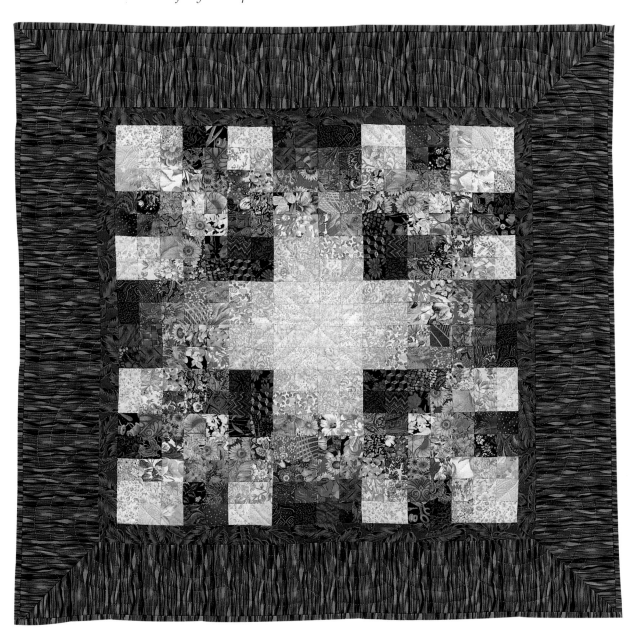

FINISHED QUILT SIZE: 40" x 40" ❖ BLOCK SIZE: 13½" ❖ BLOCK: Lasso ❖ SKILL LEVEL: Beginner

Materials

2" x 11" STRIPS

■	Dark Dark	12
▨	Light Dark	12
■	Dark Medium	16
▧	Light Medium	12
▫	Dark Light	17
□	Light Light	12

44"-WIDE FABRIC

- ⅓ yd. for inner border
- ¾ yd. for outer border
- 2¾ yds. for backing
- ⅓ yd. for binding
- 46" x 46" piece of batting

Strip Sets

Refer to "Making a Strip-Pieced Watercolor Quilt" on pages 19–25 for information on cutting and assembling strip sets and blocks.

Arrange the strips as shown below and sew them together. Make 1 of each strip set; label.

Lasso Blocks

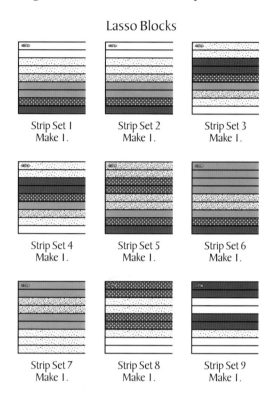

Strip Set 1
Make 1.

Strip Set 2
Make 1.

Strip Set 3
Make 1.

Strip Set 4
Make 1.

Strip Set 5
Make 1.

Strip Set 6
Make 1.

Strip Set 7
Make 1.

Strip Set 8
Make 1.

Strip Set 9
Make 1.

Block Construction

Stack the strip sets in the proper order as described on pages 23–24 and crosscut them into 4 segments, each 2" wide. Sew the segments together to make 4 blocks.

Press: U D U D U D U D U
Strip set #: 1 2 3 4 5 6 7 8 9

Lasso
Make 4.

Quilt Top Assembly

1. Arrange the blocks in 2 rows of 2 blocks each, referring to the quilt plan below and rotating the blocks as necessary. Sew the blocks together as directed in "Assembling the Quilt Top" on page 97.

Dots on the quilt plan indicate the upper left corner of the design block.

2. From the inner border fabric, cut 4 strips, each 1¾" x 42". Cut 4 strips, each 5½" x 42", from outer border fabric.
3. Sew each inner border strip to an outer border strip. Press the seam toward the outer border.
4. Measure the quilt top for borders as described in "Making Borders with Mitered Corners" on page 98. Cut the border strips to fit and stitch them to the quilt top, mitering the corners.
5. Layer the quilt top with backing and batting; baste. Quilt as desired.
6. From binding fabric, cut 4 strips, each 2½" x 42". Sew them together with a diagonal seam (page 105) to make one piece of binding that is long enough for the quilt. Bind the edges of the quilt.

PIECING FIELDS OF FAITH

by Dorothy Larsen, 1995, Naperville, Illinois, 53½" x 53½". This quilt combines warm and cool colors as well as bright and dull hues. Three-dimensional cubes seem to dance just above the quilt surface. Machine-quilted lines radiate from the center.

FINISHED QUILT SIZE: 53½" x 53½" ✧ BLOCK SIZE: 12"
BLOCKS: Goodness, Corner Lot ✧ SKILL LEVEL: Intermediate

Materials

DESIGN BLOCK	GOODNESS	CORNER LOT
Strip Size	2" x 20"	2" x 20"
	NO. OF STRIPS	
Dark Dark	11	9
Light Dark	11	13
Dark Medium	12	16
Light Medium	11	8
Dark Light	10	13
Light Light	9	5

44"-WIDE FABRIC

- ⅓ yd. for inner border
- ½ yd. for outer border
- 3⅓ yds. for backing
- ½ yd. for binding
- 59" x 59" piece of batting

Strip Sets

Refer to "Making a Strip-Pieced Watercolor Quilt" on pages 19–25 for information on cutting and assembling strip sets and blocks.

Arrange the strips as shown below and sew them together. Make 1 of each strip set for each design block; label.

Goodness Blocks

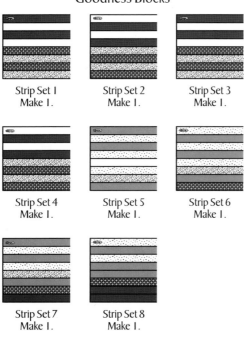

Strip Set 1
Make 1.

Strip Set 2
Make 1.

Strip Set 3
Make 1.

Strip Set 4
Make 1.

Strip Set 5
Make 1.

Strip Set 6
Make 1.

Strip Set 7
Make 1.

Strip Set 8
Make 1.

Corner Lot Blocks

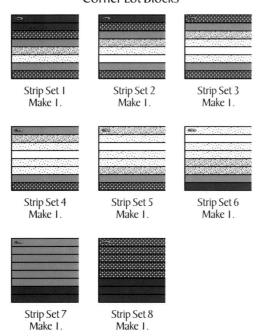

Strip Set 1
Make 1.

Strip Set 2
Make 1.

Strip Set 3
Make 1.

Strip Set 4
Make 1.

Strip Set 5
Make 1.

Strip Set 6
Make 1.

Strip Set 7
Make 1.

Strip Set 8
Make 1.

Block Construction

Stack the strip sets for the Goodness blocks in the proper order as described on pages 23–24 and crosscut them into 8 segments, each 2" wide. Repeat with the strip sets for the Corner Lot blocks. Sew the segments together to make 8 Goodness blocks and 8 Corner Lot blocks.

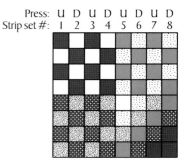

Press: U D U D U D U D
Strip set #: 1 2 3 4 5 6 7 8

Block 1
Goodness
Make 8.

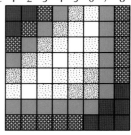

Press: U D U D U D U D
Strip set #: 1 2 3 4 5 6 7 8

Block 2
Corner Lot
Make 4.

Quilt Top Assembly

1. Arrange the blocks in 4 rows of 4 blocks each, referring to the quilt plan at right. Sew them together as directed in "Assembling the Quilt Top" on page 97.

   Dots on the quilt plan indicate the upper left corner of the design block.

2. From the inner border fabric, cut 6 strips, each 1½" x 42". Cut 6 strips, each 2" x 42", from outer border fabric.

3. Sew each inner border strip to an outer border strip. Press the seam toward the outer border strip. Cut 2 strips in half crosswise. Sew 1 piece to each of the remaining strips, using a diagonal seam as shown on pages 97–98.

4. Measure the quilt top for borders as described in "Making Borders with Mitered Corners" on page 98. Cut the border strips to fit and stitch them to the quilt top, mitering the corners.

5. Layer the quilt top with backing and batting; baste. Quilt as desired.

6. From binding fabric, cut 6 strips, each 2½" x 42". Sew them together with a diagonal seam (page 105) to make one piece of binding that is long enough for the quilt. Bind the edges of the quilt.

Taylor's Game Board

by Lorry Taylor, 1994, Mukwonago, Wisconsin, 32½" x 32½". This small wall hanging seems to be inviting viewers to play a game of checkers on the textile board. Between moves, observe the three-dimensional interplay of the dark and light values.

FINISHED QUILT SIZE: 32½" x 32½" ✦ BLOCK SIZE: 12" ✦ BLOCK: Goodness ✦ SKILL LEVEL: Beginner

Materials

2" x 13" STRIPS		
■ Dark Dark		11
▨ Light Dark		11
▨ Dark Medium		12
▨ Light Medium		11
▨ Dark Light		10
□ Light Light		9

44"-WIDE FABRIC

- ■ ¼ yd. for inner border
- ■ ⅓ yd. for outer border
- ■ 1⅛ yds. for backing
- ■ ⅓ yd. for binding
- ■ 38" x 38" piece of batting

Strip Sets

Refer to "Making a Strip-Pieced Watercolor Quilt" on pages 19–25 for information on cutting and assembling strip sets and blocks.

Arrange the strips as shown below and sew them together. Make 1 of each strip set; label.

Goodness Blocks

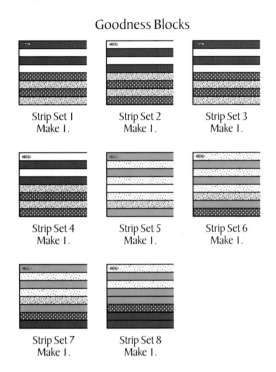

Strip Set 1
Make 1.

Strip Set 2
Make 1.

Strip Set 3
Make 1.

Strip Set 4
Make 1.

Strip Set 5
Make 1.

Strip Set 6
Make 1.

Strip Set 7
Make 1.

Strip Set 8
Make 1.

Block Construction

Stack the strip sets in the proper order as described on pages 23–24 and crosscut 4 segments, each 2" wide. Reserve the remaining portion of the strip sets. Sew the segments together to make 4 Goodness blocks.

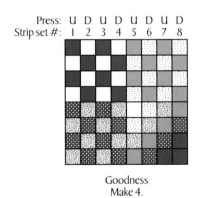

Press: U D U D U D U D
Strip set #: 1 2 3 4 5 6 7 8

Goodness
Make 4.

Quilt Top Assembly

1. Arrange the blocks in 2 rows of 2 blocks each, referring to the quilt plan below and rotating the blocks as necessary. Sew the blocks together as directed in "Assembling the Quilt Top" on page 97.

Dots on the quilt plan indicate the upper left corner of the design block.

2. From the inner border fabric, cut 4 strips, each 1½" x 42". Cut 4 strips, each 2½" x 42", from outer border fabric.

3. Measure the quilt top for borders as described in "Making Borders with Straight-Cut Corners" on page 99. Cut 2 inner side border strips to fit and stitch them to opposite side edges of the quilt top. Repeat for the inner top and bottom borders.

4. From each of the reserved strip sets, crosscut 1 segment, 1½" wide. Sew pairs of segments together, end to end, to make 4 long strips. Cut additional segments as necessary and sew them to the pieced border strips to make each of them long enough to fit the quilt. Measure the quilt as described for the inner border and add these pieced border strips to opposite side edges first, then to the top and bottom edges of the quilt top.

5. Measure, trim, and sew the outer pieced border strips to the quilt top as described for the inner border.

6. Layer the quilt top with backing and batting; baste. Quilt as desired.

7. From binding fabric, cut 4 strips, each 2½" x 42". Sew them together with a diagonal seam (page 105) to make one piece of binding that is long enough for the quilt. Bind the edges of the quilt.

$\mathscr{B}$UTTERFLIES IN THE GARDEN

by Karen Palese, 1994, Westmont, Illinois, 54½" x 65". Bright orange warms the cool jewel colors. Butterflies flutter about in the hand quilting. Light and dark three-dimensional bands lie just above the surface. The contrast in value combined with the color is wonderful.

FINISHED QUILT SIZE: 54½" x 65" ✦ BLOCK SIZE: 10½" ✦ BLOCK: Eventual ✦ SKILL LEVEL: Beginner

Materials

2" x 42" STRIPS*		44"-WIDE FABRIC

▨ Dark Dark	17	
▥ Light Dark	8	
▦ Dark Medium	6	
▨ Light Medium	4	
⬚ Dark Light	2	
☐ Light Light	12	

- ½ yd. for inner border
- ⅞ yd. for outer border
- 3⅓ yds. for backing
- ½ yd. for binding
- 60" x 71" piece of batting

*If any of the strips are less than 42" long, sew another piece to the end of the strip to make it long enough.

Strip Sets

Refer to "Making a Strip-Pieced Watercolor Quilt" on pages 19–25 for information on cutting and assembling strip sets and blocks.

Arrange the strips as shown below and sew them together. Make 1 of each strip set; label.

Eventual Blocks

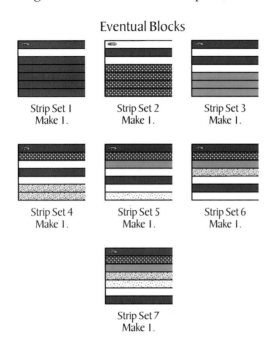

Strip Set 1
Make 1.

Strip Set 2
Make 1.

Strip Set 3
Make 1.

Strip Set 4
Make 1.

Strip Set 5
Make 1.

Strip Set 6
Make 1.

Strip Set 7
Make 1.

Block Construction

Stack the strip sets in the proper order as described on pages 23–24 and crosscut them into 20 segments, each 2" wide. Sew the segments together to make 20 blocks.

Press: U D U D U D U
Strip set #: 1 2 3 4 5 6 7

Eventual
Make 20.

Quilt Top Assembly

1. Arrange the blocks in 4 rows of 5 blocks each, referring to the quilt plan below. Sew the blocks together as directed in "Assembling the Quilt Top" on page 97.

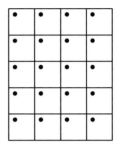

Dots on the quilt plan indicate the upper left corner of the design block.

2. From the inner border fabric, cut 6 strips, each 2½" x 42". Cut 6 strips, each 4½" x 42", from outer border fabric.
3. Measure the quilt top for borders as described in "Making Borders with Straight-Cut Corners" on page 99. Cut 2 inner border strips to fit and stitch them to opposite sides of the quilt top. Measure the quilt top for top and bottom borders, trim 2 strips to fit, and sew them to the top and bottom edges of the quilt top.
4. Repeat step 3 for the outer borders.
5. Layer the quilt top with backing and batting; baste. Quilt as desired.
6. From binding fabric, cut 6 strips, each 2½" x 42". Sew them together with a diagonal seam (page 105) to make one piece of binding that is long enough for the quilt. Bind the edges of the quilt.

CELESTIAL STARSHIP

by Deanna Spingola, 1994, Woodridge, Illinois, 38" x 38". The sense of motion on the quilt surface was achieved by using light and dark values to create depth and interest. Whirl through visual space in this watercolor spaceship.

FINISHED QUILT SIZE: 38" x 38" ⟐ BLOCK SIZE: 10½"
BLOCKS: Seville, Eventual, Deseret ⟐ SKILL LEVEL: Beginner

Materials

DESIGN BLOCK	SEVILLE	EVENTUAL	DESERET
Size	2" x 11"	2" x 11"	2" x 2"
	NO. OF STRIPS		
Dark Dark	13	17	12
Light Dark	11	8	0
Dark Medium	9	6	8
Light Medium	7	4	12
Dark Light	5	2	12
Light Light	4	12	5

44"-WIDE FABRIC

- ½ yd. for border
- 1¼ yds. for backing
- ⅓ yd. for binding
- 42" x 42" piece of batting

Strip Sets

Refer to "Making a Strip-Pieced Watercolor Quilt" on pages 19–25 for information on cutting and assembling strip sets and blocks.

Arrange the strips as shown below and sew them together. Make 1 of each strip set for each design block; label.

Seville Blocks

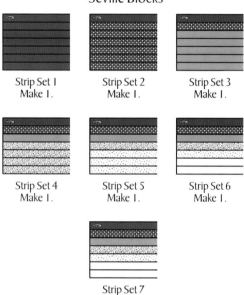

Strip Set 1
Make 1.

Strip Set 2
Make 1.

Strip Set 3
Make 1.

Strip Set 4
Make 1.

Strip Set 5
Make 1.

Strip Set 6
Make 1.

Strip Set 7
Make 1.

Eventual Blocks

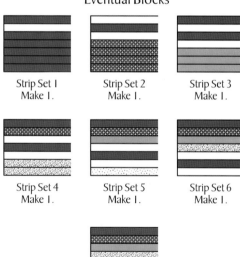

Strip Set 1
Make 1.

Strip Set 2
Make 1.

Strip Set 3
Make 1.

Strip Set 4
Make 1.

Strip Set 5
Make 1.

Strip Set 6
Make 1.

Strip Set 7
Make 1.

Block Construction

Stack the strip sets for the Seville blocks in the proper order as described on pages 23–24 and crosscut them into 4 segments, each 2" wide. Repeat with the strip sets for the Eventual block. Sew the segments together to make 4 Seville blocks and 4 Eventual blocks. Sew the 2" squares together to make 1 Deseret block.

Press: U D U D U D U
Strip set #: 1 2 3 4 5 6 7

Block 1
Seville
Make 4.

Press: U D U D U D U
Strip set #: 1 2 3 4 5 6 7

Block 2
Eventual
Make 4.

Press: U D U D U D U
Strip set #: 1 2 3 4 5 6 7

Block 3
Deseret
Make 1.

Quilt Top Assembly

1. Arrange the blocks in 3 rows of 3 blocks each, referring to the quilt plan at right. Sew them together as directed in "Assembling the Quilt Top" on page 97.

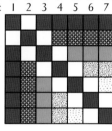

Dots on the quilt plan indicate the upper left corner of the design block.

2. From border fabric, cut 4 strips, each 3½" x 42".
3. Measure the quilt top for borders as described in "Making Borders with Mitered Corners" on page 98. Cut the border strips to fit and stitch them to the quilt top, mitering the corners.
4. Layer the quilt top with backing and batting; baste. Quilt as desired.
5. From binding fabric, cut 4 strips, each 2½" x 42". Sew them together with a diagonal seam (page 105) to make one piece of binding that is long enough for the quilt. Bind the edges of the quilt.

GABRIELLA'S GARDEN

by Deanna Spingola, 1994, Woodridge, Illinois, 36" x 36". Dark fabric fences create a token barrier around the bright, warm garden of sunshine and flowers.

FINISHED QUILT SIZE: 36" x 36" ❖ BLOCK SIZE: 18"
BLOCK: Twelve Square One ❖ SKILL LEVEL: Intermediate

Materials

2" x 11" STRIPS			44"-WIDE FABRIC
■ Dark Dark	59		■ 1⅛ yds. for backing
▦ Light Dark	11		■ ⅓ yd. for binding
▨ Dark Medium	29		■ 40" x 40" piece of batting
░ Light Medium	13		
░ Dark Light	23		
□ Light Light	9		

Strip Sets

Refer to "Making a Strip-Pieced Watercolor Quilt" on pages 19–25 for information on cutting and assembling strip sets and blocks.

Arrange the strips as shown below and sew them together. Make 1 of each strip set; label.

Twelve Square One Blocks

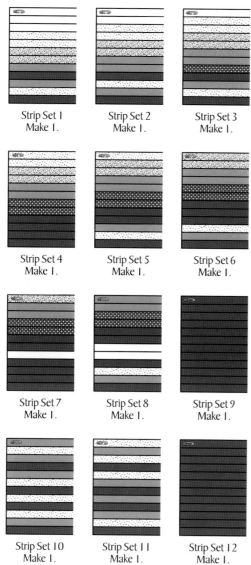

Strip Set 1
Make 1.

Strip Set 2
Make 1.

Strip Set 3
Make 1.

Strip Set 4
Make 1.

Strip Set 5
Make 1.

Strip Set 6
Make 1.

Strip Set 7
Make 1.

Strip Set 8
Make 1.

Strip Set 9
Make 1.

Strip Set 10
Make 1.

Strip Set 11
Make 1.

Strip Set 12
Make 1.

Block Construction

Stack the strip sets in the proper order as described on pages 23–24 and crosscut them into 4 segments, each 2" wide. Sew the segments together to make 4 blocks.

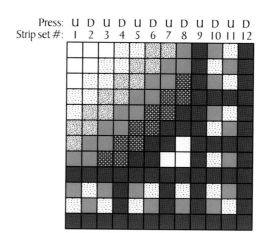

Press: U D U D U D U D U D U D
Strip set #: 1 2 3 4 5 6 7 8 9 10 11 12

Twelve Square One
Make 4.

Quilt Top Assembly

1. Arrange the blocks in 2 rows of 2 blocks each, referring to the quilt plan below and rotating the blocks as necessary. Sew them together as directed in "Assembling the Quilt Top" on page 97.

Dots on the quilt plan indicate the upper left corner of the design block.

2. Layer the quilt top with backing and batting; baste. Quilt as desired.
3. From binding fabric, cut 4 strips, each 2½" x 42". Sew them together with a diagonal seam (page 105) to make one piece of binding that is long enough for the quilt. Bind the edges of the quilt.

Creative option: Appliqué leaves scattered at random on the surface of the quilt. See "Falling Leaves" on page 3. Leaf patterns are from *Botanical Wreaths* by Laura Munson Reinstatler.

AZTEC TREASURES

by Trisha Horner, 1995, Normal, Illinois, 79½" x 79½". Echoes of ancient voices seem to transcend both time and space in this colorful quilt.

FINISHED QUILT SIZE: 79½" x 79½"   ❖   BLOCK SIZE: 18"   ❖   BLOCK: Montezuma   ❖   SKILL LEVEL: Intermediate

Materials

2" X 36" STRIPS

■	Dark Dark	21
▦	Light Dark	22
▨	Dark Medium	25
░	Light Medium	26
⬚	Dark Light	27
□	Light Light	23

44"-WIDE FABRIC

- ½ yd. for inner border
- ¾ yd. for outer border
- 4¾ yds. for backing
- ⅝ yd. for binding
- 84" x 84" piece of batting

Strip Sets

Refer to "Making a Strip-Pieced Watercolor Quilt" on pages 19–25 for information on cutting and assembling strip sets and blocks.

Arrange the strips as shown below and sew them together. Make 1 of each strip set; label.

Montezuma Blocks

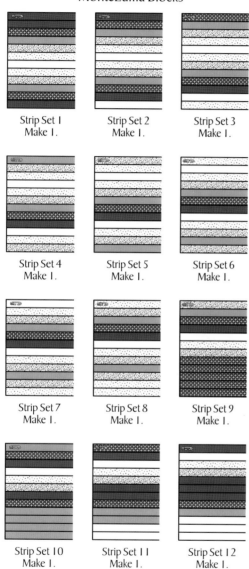

Strip Set 1
Make 1.

Strip Set 2
Make 1.

Strip Set 3
Make 1.

Strip Set 4
Make 1.

Strip Set 5
Make 1.

Strip Set 6
Make 1.

Strip Set 7
Make 1.

Strip Set 8
Make 1.

Strip Set 9
Make 1.

Strip Set 10
Make 1.

Strip Set 11
Make 1.

Strip Set 12
Make 1.

Block Construction

Stack the strip sets in the proper order as described on pages 23–24 and crosscut them into 16 segments, each 2" wide. Sew the segments together to make 16 blocks.

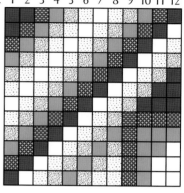

Press: U D U D U D U D U D U D
Strip set #: 1 2 3 4 5 6 7 8 9 10 11 12

Montezuma
Make 16.

Quilt Top Assembly

1. Arrange the blocks in 4 rows of 4 blocks each, referring to the quilt plan below and rotating the blocks as necessary. Sew the blocks together as directed in "Assembling the Quilt Top" on page 97.

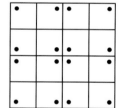

Dots on the quilt plan indicate the upper left corner of the design block.

2. From the inner border fabric, cut 8 strips, each 1½" x 42". Cut 8 strips, each 3 " x 42", from outer border fabric.

3. Sew each inner border strip to an outer border strip. Press the seam toward the outer border strip. Sew 2 of the resulting border strips together, using a diagonal seam as shown on pages 97–98. Repeat with the remaining strips to make 4 border strips.

4. Measure the quilt top for borders as described in "Making Borders with Mitered Corners" on page 98. Cut the border strips to fit and stitch them to the quilt top, mitering the corners.

5. Layer the quilt top with backing and batting; baste. Quilt as desired.

6. From binding fabric, cut 7 strips, each 2½" x 42". Sew them together with a diagonal seam (page 105) to make one piece of binding that is long enough for the quilt. Bind the edges of the quilt.

FINISHING UP

After completing the blocks for your quilt, you are ready to sew them together, add borders if desired, and prepare for quilting. Follow the directions in this section to complete your strip-pieced watercolor quilt.

Assembling the Quilt Top

1. Arrange all the blocks as shown in the quilt plan, rotating them to the proper position as necessary. Determine the best direction to press the vertical seams and press them flat.
2. Sew the blocks together in rows. Press the seams between the blocks in opposite directions from row to row. Sew the rows together. Trim all stray threads from the back.

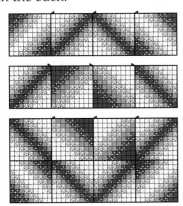

Sew blocks together.

3. Make certain that opposite edges of your quilt are the same length by folding the quilt in half lengthwise to check the sides and then crosswise to check the top and bottom edges. If opposite edges are uneven, press the seams again to remove any tucks, and square up the unequal sides.

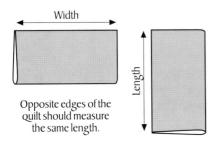

Opposite edges of the quilt should measure the same length.

Adding Borders

I prefer to use a dark border or a dark binding (or both) on strip-pieced watercolor quilts. It helps to contain the design, much as a black outline does on a drawing. Some of the quilts in this book do not have separate borders.

Should you decide to add a border to a watercolor quilt, choose one that is uncomplicated unless it is a significant design element as it is in "Celestial Starship" on page 91. A watercolor quilt contains plenty of energy and movement and doesn't need an intricate border to enhance the design.

Each quilt plan includes border measurements that correspond to the quilt pictured. The strip measurements are long enough to make borders with mitered corners where they are suggested.

Cutting and Preparing Border Strips

Cut fabric strips for borders across the width of the fabric (cross grain) and piece them together if necessary. To piece border strips, place the two strips, right sides together, at a 90° angle. Position the ¼" line of the ruler at the intersection of the two strips and trim them as shown. Pin the trimmed edge, then sew the two pieces together, using a ¼"-wide seam allowance. Press the seams open.

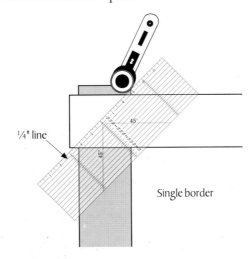

¼" line

Single border

If your quilt has more than one border, sew border strips together to make one wider border strip. To make the border strip longer, arrange pairs of strips as shown, matching the intersecting seam lines. Stitch the seam, trim the excess, and press the seam open.

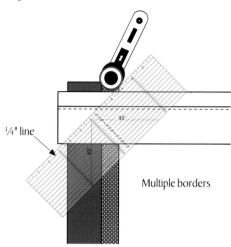

¼" line

Multiple borders

Making Borders with Mitered Corners

Many of the quilts shown have mitered corners; some have straight-cut corners. Both styles are appropriate. Choose the method you prefer.

To add mitered borders, measure the length and width of the quilt through the center. Measure the border width and double that number, add 4", then add the total to the quilt dimension. Cut border strips to those measurements.

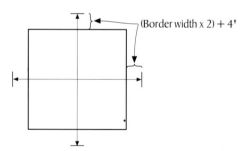

(Border width x 2) + 4"

To attach the borders:

1. Measure the length of the quilt top through the center. Mark the center and the edge measurement of the quilt top onto the border strips. Pin the two side border strips to the quilt top, matching the center and edge marks. Stitch the border strips to the quilt top, starting and stopping your

stitching ¼" away from the raw edge of the quilt top. Press seam allowances toward the border.

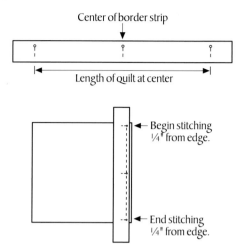

Center of border strip

Length of quilt at center

← Begin stitching ¼" from edge.

← End stitching ¼" from edge.

2. Measure the width of the quilt top through the center, without including the borders. Mark, pin, and stitch the top and bottom borders to the quilt top as you did the sides. Press the seam allowances toward the borders.

3. To miter the first corner, place it on a flat surface with the wrong side facing up. Arrange the two border strips, one on top of the other, so that they are at a 90° angle to each other. Draw a line from the stitching line in the corner to the intersection of the two border strips. Rearrange the border strips so that the bottom strip is on top; draw a stitching line as you did for the first one.

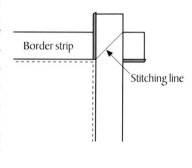

Border strip

Stitching line

4. Fold the quilt as shown. Pin the two border strips together, matching the stitching lines. Begin stitching ¼" away from the corner, at the end of the previous stitching line, and follow the stitching line to the opposite corner. Trim the seam allowances to ½" and press the seam open. Repeat for the remaining three corners.

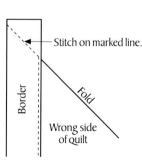

Stitch on marked line.

Border

Fold

Wrong side of quilt

Making Borders
with Straight-Cut Corners

1. Measure the center of the quilt lengthwise. Cut two side border strips to that measurement. Fold the border strips in half and then in quarters. Mark each division. Repeat with the quilt top. Pin the border strips to the quilt top, matching the markings. Sew the side border strips to the quilt, easing as necessary. Press the seam allowances toward the border.

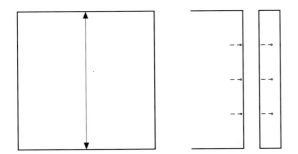

2. Measure the center of the quilt top crosswise, including the attached side border strips. Cut two border strips to that measurement. Fold and mark the border strips and the edge of the quilt top as before. Pin the border strips to the quilt top, matching the markings. Sew the border strips to the top and bottom of the quilt top, easing if necessary. Press seam allowances toward the border.

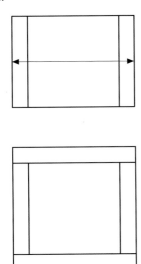

If you are adding several straight-cut borders to your quilt, do not sew them together before you attach them. Add each border independently.

Preparing to Quilt

Study the quilt to determine the most appropriate way of quilting it. Observe the internal motion, desired message, or feeling of the quilt. Choose a quilting pattern that emphasizes these ideas, or use one that complements the design block.

If marking is absolutely necessary, do it prior to layering the quilt. Mark straight lines with masking tape after the quilt is layered. Remove the tape promptly after quilting to prevent tape residue from damaging your quilt.

Various products are available to mark your quilt. If you do not plan to launder the quilt immediately, use a marking method that does not require washing to remove it.

Backing and Batting

Always use 100% cotton fabric. Plan on 40" of usable fabric width from 44"-wide fabric. Buy enough backing fabric so that the backing will be 4" to 6" larger than the quilt top.

If your quilt top is wider than 40", purchase extra-wide cotton fabric or piece the quilt backing. If it is necessary to piece the backing, remove the selvages and sew two widths of fabric together. Position the seam in the center of the quilt, or cut one of the pieces in half lengthwise and sew one piece to each side of the full width. The seams may run either vertically or horizontally. Figure the fabric requirements and use the method that requires the least amount of fabric. Press the seam allowances open.

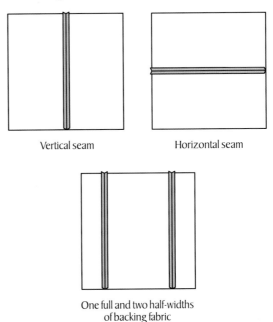

Vertical seam   Horizontal seam

One full and two half-widths
of backing fabric

You may also create a quilt backing from scraps, leftover blocks from your quilt, or strips and other pieces added to one edge of a width of fabric. Make certain the grain lines are the same for all pieces in your backing.

I often use several different, even unrelated, fabrics for the backing. Position the seam lines of the pieced backing away from the seam lines of the quilt top to reduce bulk, especially if you are a hand quilter.

Select batting according to the ultimate use of the quilt and the method of quilting. Thinner batting works best for wall quilts or hand-quilted quilts. Consider a thicker, warmer batting if you are making a bed quilt.

Cut the batting to the size suggested in the quilt pattern. To remove creases, place it in the clothes dryer with a damp towel for about fifteen minutes. Remove immediately after the dryer has stopped.

Layering the Quilt

Basting the quilt top, batting, and backing together prevents the layers from shifting during the quilting process. There are three suitable methods of basting: pin basting, tack basting, or thread basting. Any of the three is appropriate for hand quilting. Use pin or tack basting if you plan to machine quilt.

1. Mark the center of each of the four edges of the quilt backing with a straight pin.

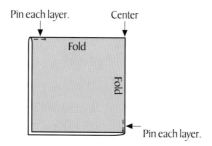

2. Select a flat, clean surface or table in a well-lit area. Use binder clips to secure the quilt backing to the table. The edge of the table must accommodate the style of clamp being used. I use a 40" x 72" cutting table and 2" clamps. Protect the table surface from possible pin or tack-needle abuse by placing a rotary mat under the backing and sliding it to a new location as you work.
3. This method for marking your basting table is from *Watercolor Quilts* by Pat Maixner Magaret and Donna Ingram Slusser. Tape a round toothpick to the center of each side and each end of the table to create a ridge you can feel through all layers of the fabric and batting.

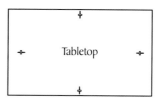

4. Fold the backing in half and lay it, wrong side up, on the table, aligning the center markings with the toothpick.

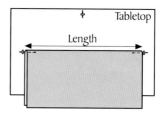

5. Smooth the backing so there are no wrinkles. Let the excess backing fabric hang over the ends and sides of the table. Clamp the sides with binder clamps, working on opposite sides in turn. Don't stretch or distort the quilt backing. If the backing fabric is either too narrow or too short to clamp to the table, use 2"-wide masking tape. Tape the backing fabric to the table, gently pulling it taut, one side at a time.

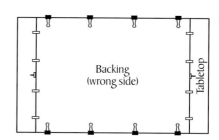

6. Mark the center of each side of the batting by folding it in quarters. Lay it on top of the backing, aligning the centers. Carefully smooth it without stretching it.
7. Mark the centers of each side of the quilt top. Unfold the top and lay it on top of the batting, right side up. Be sure to align all the centers. Smooth any fullness toward the sides and corners.

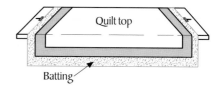

8. Baste all three layers together using one of the following methods:

- To pin-baste, use 1" or 1½" nickel-plated, rust-proof safety pins. Begin pinning in the center and gradually work to the outside edges, smoothing out any fullness. Pin every 3" to 4". Avoid pinning where any quilting lines are marked. Pin as much of the quilt as possible. Remove the clamps and shift the quilt as necessary. Continue pinning until the entire quilt is basted.

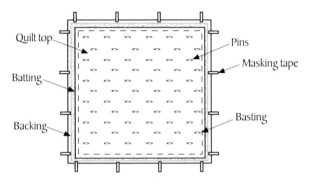

- To tack-baste, use the QuilTak tool (page 9). It secures the top, batting, and quilt backing together by inserting a short, plastic tab through the three layers. These tabs are fast to insert and easy to remove; simply cut the plastic, preferably from the back of the quilt.

   Cover your work surface with a rotary mat while tacking because the needle of this gun grazes it. Slide a yardstick under the quilt layers to move the mat when necessary. You can also use the QuilTak Basting Grid (page 9). Follow the package directions.
- To thread baste, secure the layers with straight pins first. Then thread a long needle with white thread and stitch vertical and horizontal rows about 5" apart. Remove the straight pins as you proceed. Baste diagonal lines from corner to corner and around the perimeter of the quilt. Remove the basting stitches as you quilt.

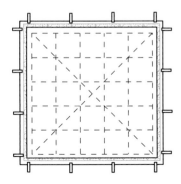

Quilting

Many of us seem to create and collect tops rather quickly, but we fall behind when it comes to quilting them. It must be an inherited characteristic, because our grandmothers did this too.

While hand quilting is traditional, machine quilting has gained general acceptance—thank goodness. Unless you are a marathon hand quilter, it is obviously much faster to machine quilt. Both have merit depending on their application. I have found that machine quilting is an acceptable way to finish any type of quilt.

Even though the major focus of strip-pieced watercolor quilts is the blending and positioning of value, quilting enhances the design and adds dimension and depth. Don't be stingy with the stitches, whether by machine or by hand. A minimum of quilting looks just exactly like what it is, a minimum.

Another advantage of adequate quilting is that the stitches stabilize the fabric so it will shrink less, which may be important if you have not prewashed your fabric but plan to wash the quilt. Large, unquilted areas of unwashed fabric are apt to shrink noticeably, distorting the quilt.

Consistent quilting is as important as adequate quilting. Since quilting draws the fabric up, it is important to quilt evenly over the surface of the quilt. If you quilt heavily in one section of the quilt and further apart in another section, the quilt will become distorted. You can also use additional quilting to help correct other problem areas.

Machine Quilting

- For machine quilting, use a clean, dependable, hard-working sewing machine. Differences in the loft of some battings may require changing the tension settings, so you should be comfortable doing this.
- Test your tension using scrap fabric and batting similar to the fabric in your quilt. Use a contrasting color in the bobbin. If you see the bobbin thread on the top of the quilt, loosen the tension until you no longer see the bobbin thread.
- Use good-quality monofilament nylon or polyester thread in the top of the machine and 100% mercerized cotton thread in a color that matches the backing in the bobbin. Do not use nylon thread in the bobbin.
- Set the stitch length for 8 to 10 stitches per inch for machine-guided quilting.
- Choose a needle size according to the weight and

style of batting; size 70/10 or 80/12 works best for machine quilting. Use a larger needle, 90/14 or 100/16, when using specialty threads, such as metallic, in the top of the machine. Begin a new project with a new needle; change machine needles after about six hours of continuous sewing, or when you hear it pop or thud into the fabric.

- A walking or even-feed foot works best for straight-line quilting because all three layers move at the same speed, preventing unevenness in the layers. Be prepared to shift and pivot the quilt when using straight-line quilting. This is fine when you are quilting a small quilt but can be more challenging for a large quilt.

- For free-motion quilting, use a darning foot, preferably one with an open toe. Drop or cover the feed dogs. Check your sewing-machine manual for information on how to do this. With free-motion quilting, you change the direction of the stitching by moving the quilt up, down, left, or right. Pivoting is unnecessary. It takes a little practice to develop a rhythm and a consistent stitch length. Use free-motion quilting for curved designs, outlining motifs, and stippling or meandering. It is not appropriate for long, straight lines of quilting.

Although stippling is often used as background quilting, I use it regularly as an allover quilting pattern for watercolor quilts. Like fingerprints, each individual seems to develop his/her own unique "stipple print." You can vary the scale of the pattern—from tiny seersucker-like stipple quilting to large-scale meandering. Adjust the scale, depending on the look you want to achieve as well as the fabric you are quilting. A small-scale stipple might be very appropriate for small-scale prints.

- Divide the quilt into workable sections. A section might consist of four smaller blocks or one large block. Stitch in-the-ditch around the outside of each section, then stitch inside each unit. Quilt section by section. Support the sections of the quilt that you are not quilting with extra tables or chairs.

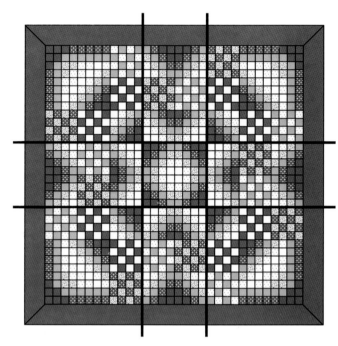

Divide the quilt into workable sections.

- Begin quilting in the center of the quilt if possible and work toward the outside edge. Position the quilt under the needle and use the hand wheel to drop the needle. Bring the bobbin thread to the top of the quilt; this prevents tangling of the thread on the back of the quilt. Hold both threads to the back of the needle as you begin to stitch. Decrease the stitch length to about 20 stitches per inch as you begin, whether in free-motion or machine-guided straight stitching, then gradually increase the length to about 8 to 10 stitches per inch. As you approach the end of a line of stitching, decrease the stitch length again to about 20 stitches per inch.

Start

Finish

Hand Quilting

Hand quilting has some definite advantages. You can take it with you if it is small enough. You don't become shackled to a sewing machine for hours, possibly away from where the family action is. While this isolation may occasionally be welcome, it can also be lonely.

I learned to hand quilt on a huge frame that filled an entire room. What might have been a somewhat overwhelming task became a wonderful social event. You can also hand quilt in a hoop; several different sizes and styles are available.

- For hand quilting, learn to wear a thimble on the middle finger of your sewing hand. Use Betweens quilting needles. See page 9.
- Thread the needle with approximately 18" to 20" of thread. Longer lengths become tangled. Make a knot at one end. Insert the needle into the quilt top and batting—but not through the backing—about 1" from the starting point. Bring the needle out at the starting point and tug gently to pull the knot through the fabric to the inside. The knot will become embedded inside the quilt. Backstitch, then quilt with a small, even running stitch through all three layers.

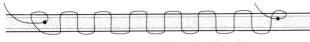

Starting and ending the quilting thread.

- Gather 3 to 4 stitches on your needle. Position your free hand under the quilt to work with your sewing hand and stitch with a rocking motion. The point of the needle should touch (gently stab) the tip of your finger with each stitch.

- Bury a knot at the end of the quilting line. Make a small knot near the last stitch, then backstitch; insert the needle into the top and batting and gently tug to pop the knot through the top layer.

Adding a Hanging Sleeve

Use a sleeve on the back of a quilt to hang it rather than using pins or tacks. You can add a permanent sleeve as you quilt the quilt.

1. Machine quilt the main body of the quilt. Determine on which edge to attach the sleeve. Stitch in-the-ditch between the border and the quilt top on the other three sides.

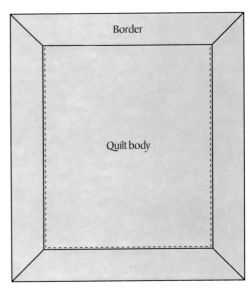

Stitch in-the-ditch around 3 sides.

2. On the back of the quilt, draw a line connecting the end of the two side-border stitching lines.

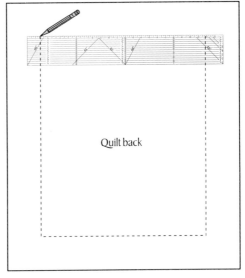

Connect the ends of the stitching lines with a pencil line.

3. Measure the quilt between the borders. Add 2" to this measurement. Measure the distance between the border and the top edge of the quilt. Add 3" to this measurement. Cut the sleeve strip according to those measurements. Use excess backing fabric for the sleeve if you have it.

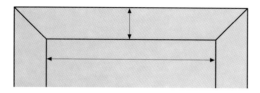

4. Turn under ½" at both short edges of the sleeve and press. Turn under ½" again and stitch.

5. Lay the sleeve, right side down, on the back of the quilt. Position the long unfinished edge of the sleeve ½" above the drawn line. Pin in place, keeping the heads of the pins closest to the edge of the quilt for easy removal as you sew. Turn the quilt right side up and stitch in-the-ditch around the last side of the border, sewing through all layers.

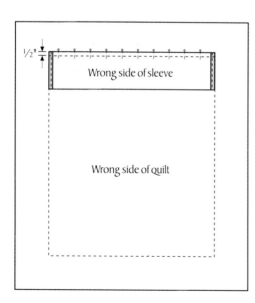

6. Pin the attached sleeve out of the way of the outer border. Finish quilting the border if necessary and trim excess fabric even with the top edge. Fold the sleeve so that the long raw edge is at the top of the quilt. Smooth out any fullness and pin the sleeve to the top edge of the quilt. Pin the binding in place. Stitch through all layers to secure the sleeve and binding. See pages 105–106.

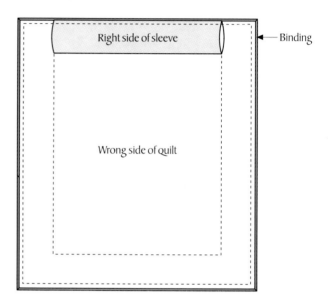

7. Insert a wooden lattice strip through the sleeve and rest the exposed ends on nails or molly screws attached to the wall. The quilt will lie flush against the wall.

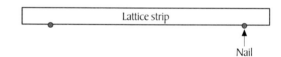

For larger quilts, make the sleeve in two sections so that the lattice strip is exposed in the center between the two sleeves. Use three nails or molly screws to support the lattice strip, one at each end and one in the middle.

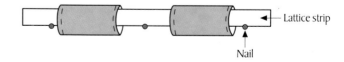

Binding and Labeling

I use straight-grain strips for binding and double-fold them because they wear better.

1. Measure around the outside edge of the quilt and add 20" for corners and joining.
2. Cut 2½"-wide strips across the width of the fabric (crosswise grain) to equal this measurement. Join the binding strips with a diagonal seam.

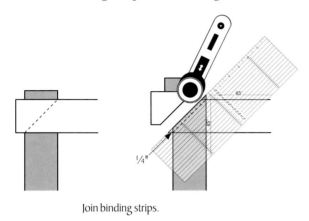

Join binding strips.

3. Press all seam allowances open. Fold the binding lengthwise with wrong sides together; press.

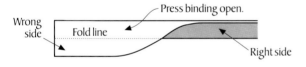

4. Open the binding strip at the beginning and fold the corner to make a 45° angle. Refold.

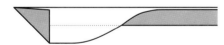

5. Walk the binding around the quilt with your fingers to be sure that the seams of the binding will not be on the corners of the quilt. When you are satisfied with the placement, position the binding on the right side of the quilt and pin it in place if desired. Leaving the first 5" unsewn, sew the binding to the right side of the quilt, using a ¼"-wide seam allowance. Use a walking foot to prevent the binding from stretching or distorting the edge of the quilt.

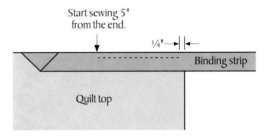

6. Stop stitching ¼" from the corner. Leave the needle down and turn the quilt so you are ready to stitch down the next side; backstitch off the edge. Clip the threads.

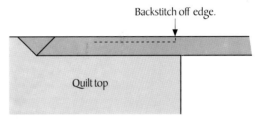

7. Fold the binding strip up and away from the corner, then fold it back down and even with the next edge. This creates a pleat in the binding.

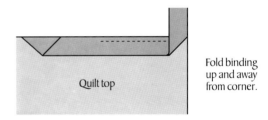

8. Make sure the pleat is straight and even with the edge of the quilt. Pin in place. Begin stitching at the edge and sew through all layers. Repeat with the remaining edges and corners.

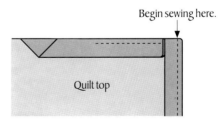

9. Stop sewing several inches away from the starting point and leave both the foot and the needle in the down position. Open the fold you made at the beginning. Tuck the end of the binding strip into the fold to determine how much excess fabric needs to be trimmed away. Cut the excess fabric from the end of the strip, but don't remove too much. Tuck the end of the strip back under the beginning. Sew through all layers, enclosing the end of the binding under the beginning of the strip.

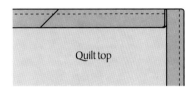

10. Turn the folded edge of the binding over the raw edge of the quilt and pin it to the back. Hand stitch the binding to the back, mitering each corner. If you prefer, machine stitch the binding in place by stitching in-the-ditch from the front of the quilt. Stitch the corners carefully to make certain that you catch the binding on each side.

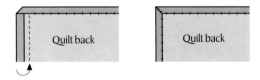

Attach a label to the back of the quilt and prepare for the applause! Celebrate by selecting your favorite fat-filled delicacy from the fifth major food group—chocolate. Yes, it's okay to reward yourself occasionally with food as well as fabric, but then it's back to the fat-free SnackWell's® for me.

MEET THE AUTHOR

GARY PETERSON

Deanna Spingola grew up in California and bought her first sewing machine at the age of twelve. A seventh-grade sewing class inspired her to save her baby-sitting money for the purchase. From that point on, she constructed most of her own clothes. Later, she sewed for her husband and children.

What began as a worthwhile hobby later became a career. She attended school in California and, over the years, taught many different sewing and design classes, including basic sewing, pattern alterations and design, and tailoring. Long before the advent of the rotary cutter, she used many of the fabric scraps from those earlier projects in her first attempt at quilting. A few years later, she had the opportunity to

really learn about the traditional methods of quilting.

Since 1987, she has been an Independent Sales Representative selling fabric, trims, and laces to fabric stores. Imagine being required to visit fabric stores every day as part of your job! Currently, she represents five trim, lace, and fabric companies. In addition, she teaches one-day quilting and heirloom sewing seminars.

Deanna enjoys cooking, creative writing, reading, sewing, and genealogical research. She has four grown children. She recently remarried, and she and her husband are living "happily ever after" in a Chicago suburb. Between them, they have six wonderful grandchildren.

That Patchwork Place Publications and Products

4", 6", 8", & metric Bias Square® • BiRangle™ • Ruby Beholder® • ScrapMaster • Rotary Rule™ • Rotary Mate™ • Bias Stripper™
Shortcuts to America's Best-Loved Quilts (video)

AMERICA'S BEST-LOVED QUILT BOOKS®

Many titles are available at your local quilt shop. For more information, send $2 for a color catalog to
That Patchwork Place, Inc., PO Box 118, Bothell WA 98041-0118 USA.

☎ U.S. and Canada, call **1-800-426-3126** for the name and location of the quilt shop nearest you.
Int'l: 1-206-483-3313   **Fax:** 1-206-486-7596   **E-mail:** info@patchwork.com   **Web:** http://oak.forest.net/patchwork   3.96